Called to Belong

Sister Stephanie Clifford

PREPARING THE MENTALLY HANDICAPPED
PERSON FOR CONFIRMATION

Kevin Mayhew Publishers

First published in Great Britain in 1984 by
KEVIN MAYHEW LTD.,
55 Leigh Road,
Leigh-on-Sea, Essex SS9 1JP.

ISBN 0 86209 057 1

ACKNOWLEDGMENTS

I wish to express my gratitude to the many mentally handicapped people who have prompted me to write this book. Special thanks go to Josephine Pitts and her catechist Dorothy Gardner, to Maggie Cox and the St Alban's group for living to the full this programme of catechesis in preparation for the sacrament of confirmation.
    I would also like to thank:
Father David Wilson, director of the Pastoral Office for Handicapped People at St Joseph's Centre who has guided and supported me during work on the programme of sessions;
Paul Gardner, Maggie Cox and Mabel Scanlon for the photographs;
Josephine Devaney for typing the manuscript;
and finally Bishop Mahon for sharing so wholeheartedly in the programme and for his encouragement.

Typeset by Barry Sarling, Rayleigh, Essex
Printed and bound by Richard Clay PLC, Bungay, Suffolk

CONTENTS

FOREWORD

To confirm a mentally handicapped person is a very special experience for a Bishop. I suspect that preparing a mentally handicapped person for the sacrament is an equally moving experience for the catechist. Reading the introductory sections of this book by Sister Stephanie has helped me to see how the mentally handicapped person can bring all of us to understand in a new and fresh way the meaning of our faith and in particular, the meaning of the sacrament of confirmation.

Working as she does in St Joseph's Centre for handicapped people, Sister Stephanie has the experience needed to produce a book for catechists of the handicapped. But her book will be of great value not only for those concerned with preparing handicapped people for confirmation, but for every catechist trying to understand and transmit the mystery of the gift of the Spirit given in the sacrament of confirmation.

When Pope John Paul visited St Joseph's Hospital for the Handicapped in Rosewell on his recent visit, he quoted a Gaelic phrase that describes the handicapped as living under God's protection, 'God's handicapped'. 'Such a sensitive description or title', the Pope said, 'captures a whole variety of profoundly Christian insights into the meaning of life and its dignity.' Sister Stephanie, in this book, helps us to gain those insights and shows us how to share them.

Perhaps I might end this foreword with the closing words of Pope John Paul's address at Rosewell: 'In drawing us to love and assist the handicapped, the Lord Jesus touches our lives with his strength, and finally rewards us according to his promise: ''as you did it to one of the least of my brethren, you did it to Me.'' '

Gerald Mahon
Bishop in West London

INTRODUCTION

This book is a response to a growing number of requests from parents, catechists and priests for help in preparing mentally handicapped people for the sacrament of confirmation. Sometimes confirmation is offered to parents as an alternative to a request for first holy communion for their handicapped child. Confirming at the age of six or seven means more often than not no preparation of child or family, and the significance of confirmation as the sacrament of belonging is lost.

Today discussion continues on the most suitable age for receiving this sacrament, but there is a tendency towards seeking greater maturity. Mentally handicapped people can only benefit from this trend. For those whose intellectual development has been slowed down, receiving confirmation at a later age means that it will have a deeper significance in their lives, and therefore in the lives of their families and the parish community. It also provides better opportunities for an appropriate catechesis. Further, although those who were confirmed at birth or at an early age are not eligible to receive the sacrament again, they would clearly benefit from sharing in the preparation with others.

Preparation for confirmation at a later age will often coincide with a significant change of circumstances for a mentally handicapped person. Leaving a special school means leaving a secure and familiar environment which has provided a sense of belonging. The adult training centre—always assuming a place is available—however good it may be, is foreign to the normal expectancy of young adults. Through a confirmation programme at this stage in the mentally handicapped person's life, the Church can restore this sense of belonging.

Many still find it difficult to see mentally handicapped people as anything other than children. Raising the age for admission to confirmation tells us, and through us, the mentally handicapped person, that the Church accepts him as a young adult.

Confirmation, like first holy communion, needs to be seen within the context of an ongoing relationship with the Lord. There is a great temptation, especially with mentally handicapped people, to just 'do the confirmation bit' and 'the first holy communion bit' and to isolate these significant events in the life of the person and of the Church from the wholeness of our religion.

Such is the richness of the sacrament of confirmation that we are obliged to choose from among the different aspects of the sacrament and the different rites contained within it. To present the mentally handicapped person with every aspect of this sacrament would hinder rather than help his preparation. The emphasis in this programme is on confirmation as *the sacrament of belonging*. For the mentally handicapped person preparation for confirmation is not so much a question of explaining but rather of enabling him to feel intuitively the Spirit of Jesus at work in his life, and in the lives of the people who surround him.

Confirmation is the sacrament of the Spirit. It is the same Spirit, who was present in Jesus, who will help the mentally handicapped person to 'understand' the ways of God and to bear witness to him in his daily life. One of the best ways of experiencing the power of the Spirit is through the context of prayer and catechesis within a believing community—a community open to welcoming the handicapped person and to sharing with him its life and its faith. Hence the stress on building community. The aim is to surround the handicapped person with adult believing people. By creating an atmosphere of genuine friendship the adult community provides the security needed by the handicapped person to feel that he is welcome and that he belongs. Within this human experience of being welcomed, called and belonging, the handicapped person will intuitively sense the living presence of Jesus and his Spirit, alive in a community of faith.

The themes of 'friendship', 'new life', 'reconciliation', and the specific section on 'waiting for the Spirit' in Part II will prepare the handicapped person in a concrete way for the reception of the sacrament of confirmation within his local parish and alongside his normal counterpart.

We need to take the confirmation and the spiritual formation of our people seriously. It will be one way of showing them that the Church cares. Through the confirmation programme they and their parents will experience the support and love of an accepting Church, and be led to grow spiritually.

FINDING THE RIGHT APPROACH

Mentally handicapped people may differ from the so called 'normal' population, but this difference is one of degree not of kind. They are developing people who are more similar to than different from us. They are just as human as you or I—limited, finite and mortal. We are each imperfect variations on the theme of being human. The handicapped person has his limitations and I have mine. Mostly he is limited in terms of abstract thinking. He thinks in a more concrete way than I do. He has his world, his perceptions, his ideas, his experiences, which are as precious to him as mine are to me. In fact, the handicapped person is often more gifted than I am in terms of emotional and affective expression and in his ability to appreciate and to enjoy the little things of life. He is much more spontaneous than I am, and in an intuitive way he is capable of contemplation, and of bringing me with him into the world of the sacred. Whether he develops concepts of right or wrong, whether he trusts others or becomes isolated from them, whether he strives responsibly or exploits others irresponsibly, depends mainly on the kind of environment and formation provided for him by family and Church.

Since a mentally handicapped person is someone who does not develop beyond the concrete level of understanding, a religious programme that is based on instruction will not foster growth in faith. Nevertheless, the handicapped have the right to hear the Good News. As members of the Church they have a right to the sacraments and to develop their spiritual life. For this to happen they need an approach and a programme that is sensitive to both their spiritual and psychological development. The pastoral task is always to build on the gifts of a person rather than to struggle to overcome the difficulties and deficiencies. It is amazing what can be achieved given an approach which is in keeping with their potential.

There are many ways of learning. We are more used to the way in which we draw on the principles of cause and effect. But there is another kind of learning that is more intuitive, through which we identify closely with the object or the mystery and so 'know' it. The tree has to be *my* tree before I know it. I have to live the experience if I am going to grasp what it is about. I can grasp the connection between two realities—the priest is here, Jesus is here—without a long explanation on the sacrament of ordination. The key thing is to place the realities side by side, and *to evoke* the connection between them. Once the catechist begins *to explain* the mentally handicapped person is no longer able to follow.

Words, especially abstract words, can be a stumbling block. There are other ways of communication and expression apart from speaking. There is the use of gestures. Simple every day gestures that express welcome, offering praise or an attitude of recollection speak to mentally handicapped people and help us to communicate with them. Music and song and sharing food all furnish us with powerful means of communication. All these words, actions and objects can be used in such a way that a symbolic way of learning takes place, that through them one catches something of a reality that is hidden and yet partially manifest. For example, the special reverence with which the Bible, the Book of God's Word, is handled leads you to see it as the means by which God does actually speak to us. A wholehearted gesture of welcome with words truly meant 'Jesus says to you today: "Come to me" ' will teach a person something of the attitude Jesus has towards him. Communication calls for invention and imagination. We will never exhaust the possibilities.

Catechesis with mentally handicapped people is like an extraordinary adventure which gives them the opportunity to grow humanly and spiritually—but it is a difficult adventure that we cannot undertake alone. We need to build a community of believing people. This is important for the handicapped person because then the message of the Gospel comes through the community of the faithful which is 'the Church' in miniature, as it were, and in which the mentally handicapped person has a place like all other baptised persons.

Our mission is to be witnesses to the coming of God into the life of these people, and their companions. Thus the Church, which to our mentally handicapped people will be their parents, friends, catechists, the priest, will be where they are welcomed, loved and treated like others, because of Jesus who gives value to all. This, too, is the context in which they will witness to us and so fulfil their own missionary vocation.

FAITH AND THE MENTALLY HANDICAPPED PERSON

With a more traditional approach to religious education and faith it may be difficult for us to be in tune with our mentally handicapped friends. We may be used to thinking in terms of religious knowledge or religious instruction. Our ideas may be rather abstract. We need to try and penetrate our faith at a level that is appropriate to someone less advanced than we are in intellectual development. It will be difficult if not impossible to animate the sessions in this programme without this renewed vision of what we believe. When we do this we discover that our faith life is considerably enriched.

Let us begin with the story of Zaccheus.

Jesus entered Jericho and was going through the town when a man whose name was Zaccheus made his appearance; he was one of the senior tax collectors and a wealthy man. He was anxious to see what kind of man Jesus was, but he was too short and could not see him for the crowd; so he ran ahead and climbed a tree to catch a glimpse of Jesus who was to pass that way. When Jesus reached the spot he looked up and spoke to him: 'Zaccheus, come down. Hurry, because I must stay in your house today.' And he hurried down and welcomed him joyfully. They all complained when they saw what was happening. 'He has gone to stay at a sinner's house' they said. But Zaccheus stood his ground and said to the Lord, 'Look, sir, I am going to give half my property to the poor, and if I have cheated anybody I will pay him back four times the amount.' And Jesus said to him: 'Today salvation has come to this house, because this man too is a son of Abraham, for the Son of Man has come to seek out and save what he lost.'   (*Luke 19:1-10 [JB]*)

The story starts with Jesus, Son of God. The first thing he does is to speak to Zaccheus. He does not give information, there is no doctrinal statement. He simply speaks to him as a friend. Zaccheus responds to this invitation. He hurries down and welcomes Jesus with great joy. There is fellowship in welcome, in a meal and in staying in someone else's house.

In this story there are three important elements:
God speaks. This is what we call revelation.
Then man responds. This is faith.
The interaction between these results in a union. What is revealed is not a body of doctrine, it is a person, God himself. He makes himself known by speaking to us as a friend, and living in our midst. He reveals himself as a God who says 'I will never take back my love' (*Psalm 88:33*), and 'You are mine, you are precious to me' (*Isaiah 43:4*). He is the God who loves 'the world so much that he sent his only Son' (*John 3:16*).

God reveals himself in this way so as to establish with us a relationship that is intensely personal. Jesus comes to reveal his Father so that 'the love with which you loved me may be in them, so that I may be in them' (*John 17:26*).

At the heart of our religion is a relationship with a person. Faith is not so much to do with knowledge and assenting to a doctrine. It is to do with welcoming a person. This we want to share with our mentally handicapped friends. They are at the level of relating to a person rather than knowing doctrine. If we can join them there it will be to our spiritual advantage.

This is why the basis of this Confirmation programme is growing in relationships. In a sense this is what we hope 'to teach'. But you cannot 'teach' relationships or a sense of belonging. They are much more on a level of experience so this is where we always begin, as you will see from the sessions.

We are concerned with the level of relationships and in particular the relationship with the living Lord. Our catechesis therefore does not try to pass on knowledge or a moral code. Its principal objective is to establish a relationship between the person and Christ. That relationship cannot develop without a good relationship between the mentally handicapped person and you—the catechist and friend. Your first task is to share as far as possible the life of the mentally handicapped person and to enjoy human experiences together. So the context within which catechesis is possible is that of a friendship created through the group situation. It is a demanding catechesis but one which uncovers aspects of the Gospel which are often otherwise forgotten.

COMMUNITIES OF FAITH

a. THE SIGNIFICANCE OF THE GROUP

> When Pentecost day came round, they had all met in one room, when suddenly they heard what sounded like a powerful wind from heaven, the noise of which filled the entire house in which they were sitting; and something appeared to them that seemed like tongues of fire; these separated and came to rest on the head of each of them. They were all filled with the Holy Spirit, and began to speak foreign languages as the Spirit gave them the gift of speech. *(Acts 2:1-4)*

It is quite clear from this text that the gift of the Spirit of Jesus is made to the community of believers, the Church. The *Acts of the Apostles* show that it is through the community that this gift is subsequently given to new believers. Mentally handicapped people need the experience of a community of believing people in which to prepare themselves for the meeting with the Spirit in confirmation. Through our own experience with mentally handicapped people we know that their gifts are often hidden. These hidden gifts can blossom through and within the small community of believing people. The group provides the context for gifts to be shared.

The small group is also the context in which a sense of belonging can develop and grow. Through baptism we belong to the Church. But this idea can too easily remain notional and abstract. The small community of believing people can make the sense of belonging real and concrete. Even here, the mentally handicapped person may need time and support. This is specially true when he or she, through no fault of their own, tends to be egocentric. Belonging can also be an area of struggle for the family as a whole. Parents may well ask where does their son or daughter really belong. Both parent and child can be helped to feel that sense of belonging within that small community of believing people.

Such a welcoming supportive group will provide the context for the mentally handicapped person agreeing to belong. Do we not all have to agree to make a commitment to be Christians at some point? Membership of the Church implies a decision. The decision to belong to this community of faith united to the larger Church family may be the most concrete way a mentally handicapped person can commit him or herself to the Church. It is the bishop who affirms this commitment when he confirms the mentally handicapped person. Through this anointing with the Spirit he says to mentally handicapped people 'Yes, you belong to the people of God.' The bishop, if he is to be significant in forming this sense of belonging, must be seen more as a friend than as a stranger. It is important, then, for the group to have met him before the actual celebration of confirmation.

From many points of view, then, the group situation is the ideal setting for the preparation of the sacrament of confirmation. The challenge for those of us concerned with the preparation is to build small faith communities into which mentally handicapped people can be welcomed and in which they feel they belong. We need to create communities which become, not other isolated ghettos, but rather stepping stones for integration into the larger faith community of the parish. In these groups it is the relationship between all the members of the group that becomes the vital element in the catechesis. The group itself is the vehicle for passing on the faith. What you want to teach is what you as a community are living, and so you teach by becoming a living loving community of faith-full people. The medium is the message.

b. FORMING THE GROUP

When groups of parents and friends from local parishes or deaneries meet regularly for social and liturgical events a start has already been made to form from those who attend, a small faith community. Among those who participate in such events you will find your candidates for confirmation, interested parents and volunteers prepared to act as friends. The group should not be too large, about twelve people is the recommended maximum. Drawing from people who already know each other will facilitate the formation of a community. You can quickly move on to deciding when and how you will work through the confirmation programme. It is unwise to work out a timetable that would suit every group. This is best done by the group itself. Those who are responsible need to ensure that they have grasped the section entitled *MAKING THE SES-*

SIONS WORK' before embarking on the programme.

For a group beginning from scratch I would recommend the practical booklet *Colours of Day* (available from Liverpool Catholic Social Services, 150 Brownlow Hill, Liverpool L3 5RF). It describes a well tested way of starting a group with mentally handicapped people.

It may be that you are in a situation where there is only one mentally handicapped person to be prepared for the sacrament of confirmation. A group can be very small, perhaps just three or four people. Maybe two families could link up. Mentally handicapped people who have already been confirmed could be in the group also. The possible combinations are numerous.

c. PARENTS AND PARISH

The introduction to the rite of confirmation states 'The initiation of children into the sacramental life is for the most part the responsibility and concern of Christian parents,' and it goes on to say they are expected to play an active part in the celebration of the sacrament. The parents should therefore be part of any group that is set up.

From the parish point of view, such parents must not become separated from the regular group of parents whose children are preparing for confirmation. They need to be invited to parents' meetings and to receive all necessary information about the nature of the sacrament of confirmation and how it is to be fully celebrated. The parents could also be involved in helping to develop some service programmes which would involve their children in parish activities. The regular group of parents would profit from hearing about the approach to confirmation for the mentally handicapped young people. For the confirmation service itself it is only right that mentally handicapped people, who have been prepared within the small community, join the larger parish community wherever practicable as regards numbers, time and pace of the liturgical celebration.

d. SPONSORS

The Praenotanda to the Rite of Confirmation says: 'Ordinarily there should be a sponsor for each of those to be confirmed. The sponsor brings the candidate to receive the sacrament, presents him to the minister for anointing, and will later help him to fulfil his baptismal promises faithfully under the influence of the Holy Spirit.' It is suggested in the rite that if possible the sponsor should be the baptismal Godparent. This shows the unity between the two sacraments. However, a special sponsor for confirmation may be chosen provided that they are sufficiently mature for this role, and that they belong to the Catholic community and have received all three sacraments of initiation, baptism, confirmation and the eucharist. The revised Rite of Confirmation originally allowed parents themselves to be sponsors to their child for this sacrament. However the new Code of Canon Law of 25 January 1983 has revised this and parents can no longer request or be invited to be their son's or daughter's sponsor.

In preparing the mentally handicapped person for confirmation we need to respect both his religious readiness as a person moving gradually towards God, and the initiative of the Spirit who wishes to meet the mentally handicapped person and form him into Christ. The mentally handicapped person may be limited in his ability to comprehend, but not in his ability to love. Confirmation is the sign of acceptance by the Church community and a sign of self-commitment to God in that community. A commitment to witness to Jesus and to serve him and others has important psychological and spiritual implications for mentally handicapped people. The grace of God, which seals this commitment, becomes their source of power. A catechesis developed around belonging to a faith community and the experience of the work of the Spirit in that community provides a positive programme for their spiritual development.

This whole pattern of spiritual formation has a parallel in the revised catechumenate. It provides many lessons for catechesis as a whole: the significance of the community of faith which creates an atmosphere of love, joy and security; the importance of the non-verbal; the attitudes of others; the emphasis on knowing *someone* rather than something. Some will say that this method of preparation for confirmation with mentally handicapped people is too demanding and time-consuming. It is demanding! But maybe for those so often excluded it is right to set a high standard.

MAKING THE SESSION WORK

Each session is divided into two main parts:
THE HUMAN EXPERIENCE;
and **THE SPIRITUAL DIMENSION.**
The lived experiences of the mentally handicapped person form the basis of all your work in the spiritual part of the session. It is necessary for the group to have actually lived the experience that you are talking about. Without this lived experience the session becomes irrelevant. Hence the necessity to take the time to make provision for the experiences suggested in this programme or for those most suited to your group. Plan your session so as to allow time to do things together and to share together. Take photographs or slides to mark the event or the occasion. This is really worthwhile and makes the actual catechesis, the spiritual dimension, much more meaningful for the handicapped person. The spiritual dimension section is, in fact, the core of the session. In this part of the session you begin by focusing on what you have experienced together.

Let us look at a session together to understand how it works. We will take Session 2 from Part I—*FRIENDS.*

First, the *aim* of the session in clearly stated. In this particular session, the aim is to become aware that we are happy when we are together as friends, and that when we are together in this way, Jesus is with us.

THE HUMAN EXPERIENCE is friendship: being friends, having friends, doing things together that create interaction, and so deepen friendship. The human experience element is not just a preliminary readiness exercise for the 'real' catechesis: rather the act of faith is situated within the interpretation of the human experience. The core of the session begins by recalling the lived experience.

RECALL THE HUMAN EXPERIENCE
John, I am happy that you are here tonight.
Tom, I am happy that you are here tonight.
Mary, I am happy that you are here tonight.
Address each person in the group,
individually by name,
handicapped and non-handicapped.

I want you to be happy here.
I want this place to be our special place.
I enjoy preparing it for you, John.
I enjoy preparing it for you, Tom.

Name each one as before.
Mention special things you did to get the place
ready.

Joan, when you came here last time you met Susan,
<u>your</u> special friend.
Tom, <u>you</u> met your special friend too, didn't you?
John is your special friend.

Mention each person and their special friend
and help them to begin to relate to one another.

You are happy together Mary and Tina.

Involve everyone by naming them in a similar way.

I have a photograph of you, Mary.
Look!
There is Tina.
You are enjoying yourselves!

Show photographs of the group doing something
together.

We are all enjoying ourselves.
We may have been a little afraid wondering what
would happen to us and who we were going to meet.
Now we feel better.
We have friends here.
You have many friends here, Joan.

Address each person in the same way.

Helping people to become aware of their experiences is
the beginning of the search of how God reveals himself in their
lives. One can never interpret what has not been lived in some
way. One can never interpret events that are not vividly
brought to a level of awareness, so in recalling the experience
through the use of concrete things (symbols) the events are
relived and made present again.

We must be careful, however, not to get bogged down by
the human experience. We must move on. We cannot let
people get so fascinated by recalling the experience that it fails

to provide the stepping off point for that intuitive leap which carries us beyond the visible to the invisible, that carries us beyond the Human Experience to the mystery. So we move to.

DEEPEN THE HUMAN EXPERIENCE
> <u>We</u> are all friends.
> When we meet new friends,
> people who say 'Hello, how are you?',
> people who welcome us,
> people who like us,
> we are happy, we are very happy.
> We feel good.
> We <u>want</u> to be together.
> We are happy to be together.

Here we are trying to help each one to recognise the human experience as truly his or her own, and then, to become aware that the others in the group share some aspect of that experience. So a sense of belonging together settles in. From 'I have that experience' we are now at the stage of 'We have that experience'. We are now focused on the experience in such a way that we are inside the experience and it is inside us. The leader can now verbalise how we feel about the experience, guide us to say implicitly: 'Yes, you are touching my experience', 'That is my feeling about it', 'I do appreciate it in this way and I know the others in the group do too'. A common awareness is present and the group of individuals at this point is becoming more of a *community*.

Now the moment has come for a more explicitly spiritual dimension to be brought into play. From the experience of being friends together we move to an awareness of being the people of God together, to appreciating that the Church is the people of God gathered together by his Word.

CHURCH DIMENSION
> When we are together Jesus is with us.
> When we are happy to be together Jesus is with us.
> When we come here around the Holy Book Jesus is
> with us.
> When we read from the Holy Book Jesus speaks to us.
> Jesus is with us.

Here we want to become aware that we are the Christian community gathered together around the Holy Book. We do not 'teach' Church or liturgy or life. We become aware. We want to give our people a sense of Church. We create an awareness.

PROCLAIM THE GOOD NEWS

Up to this point the leader has been recalling and evoking life, liturgy, and Church. Now she proclaims the Good News. Go slowly towards the Bible. Pick it up with reverence. For the handicapped person the important thing is that everyone is happy around the Book of God's Word. It is sacred to be this way. Jesus is with us and he is with us when we come together around the Holy Book.

> In the Holy Book Jesus says:
> 'Where two or three meet in my name,
> I shall be there with them.'   *Matthew 18-20*
> *Repeat once.*
> Jesus says:
> 'When you are together,
> I am with you.'

THE MESSAGE

The Word of God is for all people of all time. The message of the Gospel is for you today. At this moment the catechist is confronted with the heart of the Christian mission. At this moment the catechist stands before each one, holds the hands of each person in turn, or places her hands on each one's head, calls each by name and says:
'John, Jesus says to you today, I am with you.'
This is the climax of the session. The leader stands before each catechist and each handicapped person as identified with the risen Christ. Because of this she speaks the message not as something past but alive, available and given personally at this moment. A final call to faith is offered. We hope that everything leading up to this moment will have awakened people to hear the message of the Gospel and to respond.

Is this not the method Jesus used? Remember the story of the Samaritan woman. Jesus used a drink of water and his thirst to lead her to thirst for God. He moves from one level to another until his message reaches its climax.

In this phase of the session the message is expressed through song, dance or gesture. The style of the response depends on the group and on the mood of the session. Whatever form it takes should give a sense of contemplative enjoyment of the message, and it draws the explicitly spiritual part of the session to a close. The response flows from an awareness, even a vague global awareness, of the hitherto hidden connections between one's life and the God of life that have been brought to light.

A session has a very distinctive flow. We begin with the life experiences of our mentally handicapped people and catechists, and conclude with the proclamation of the Gospel. We do not explain what we are doing, we simply place realities side by side: we juxtapose our lives as they are, and the Gospel. My life is like a symbol, I interpret my life in the light of that mystery. In technical language we speak of this as the *interpretative mode*. The Gospel in my life has density and I can reach God through the symbolic level. The catechists can learn this way of interpreting his or her own life experiences as a part of their spirituality. The mentally handicapped have to be led, to be guided.

As leader-catechist you have a written session to help you. However, the written session is only a tool to be used to help focus on an aspect of the mystery to be dealt with. It is not to be followed mechanically or slavishly, least of all memorised. It is not a question of learning by heart but of entering into the feelings of the group and drawing them into the mystery. As leader you are expected to steep yourself in the mystery. Things go right or wrong in the measure that you understand the function of the written session. There are two elements for any session:

—the written text;
—the group.

In both cases you as leader have to 'get inside' the session and 'inside' the group. You need to be present to the mystery and present to the group.

Once you begin to develop certain skills you will find it easier to lead people through a session. You develop skills gradually and with experience.

A key skill you need to deveop is *poise*. Lack of poise makes people move too quickly in the session progression. Timing and pacing are key and these depend on the basic security of the group leader. The use of simple gestures is not only effective with a group but it is also effective for oneself. You can consciously slow yourself down by meaningful gestures. If you can control your gestures then you can control your pace. Eye contact must not be ignored in a session. Look at people and watch especially the eyes of the non-verbal people in your group. More can be expressed with some mentally handicapped people through eye contact and facial expression than through words.

The printed text suggests moments of silence. Treat them as suggestions. Following the text slavishly could mean putting silence in the wrong place so that you get awkward artificial pauses instead of meaningful silences. You need to develop an instinct for when to speak and when to remain silent.

The way in which you pick up or hold the Bible needs a certain presence and sense of reverence. What you have to aim at doing is to draw the group with you through your mode of presence as you pick up the Holy Book. The message of the Gospel has to be *proclaimed* and in so doing it is important not to lose the group. Memorising the message will help you to keep your group focused as you proclaim the Good News. Try not to be to wordy. Use language to create an experience and to express what is actually going on. This is one reason why you simply cannot go ploughing through the session saying *'We are all happy to be together'* if some of your group are not experiencing being happy! You are saying what is not true and your handicapped person will 'know' it. The reality for the group is that we are happy together reaching out to make our friends happy. Say what is really happening and not what the text tells you to say. Say it in such a way that it corresponds to what you feel and to what the group feels. Then you will have a symbolic progression true to the group and true to the mystery. The printed text is only an instrument to help you focus on an aspect of the mystery. Without being present to the group and to the mood of the moment everything you say or do becomes artificial.

The leader-catechist depends on the support of the other catechists in the group. They are there to prepare themselves and their friends to be open to the Word of God. They do this primarily by being totally present to what you as leader say and do. When the catechists are focused themselves they find that their friends are willing to participate and to become involved in the session. The catechists can enhance this readiness for catechesis by quietly repeating to their friends words or phrases used by the leader. They can help draw their friends into the session and into a sense of the sacred by movement, gestures and by their own spontaneous reactions. Their enthusiaism or lack of it will determine to some extent how much their friends are able to participate and to respond to God's Word.

This way of working is ideally suited to the mentally handicapped person's intellectual development. The catechesis is very contemplative in style. What we are doing is simply trying to initiate the mentally handicapped person into the mystery of Christ among us and within us through real human experiences within a community of believing people. As catechists we have to continue to grow in faith. We need to become more aware of God present in our daily lives, of living faith so that we become a *presence in faith* to our friends. We cannot 'explain' to them God's presence among us. We cannot 'explain' our faith in him. This is something that they will 'know' through us and through the example of our lives. The atmosphere of living faith is the powerhouse for growth in faith. The faith of our mentally handicapped friends will grow in proportion to the catechists' growth in faith.

PROGRAMME OF SESSIONS

This explicit religious formation programme can be adapted or changed to suit the needs of a particular group. The purpose of the following sessions is to provide a prayerful experience through which the mentally handicapped person and other members of the group experience the presence of the Spirit. As we come together to give and to receive we share *Good News*. We become holy within a community gathered together around the Book of God's Word to give praise. As we meet together to live and to share our human experiences we discover the saving power of Jesus through his Spirit. Through the life of the group and the moments spent in prayer we will *know* the Spirit as God's gift to us. The fruits of the Spirit in the life of each of us give glory to God. We will prepare ourselves to receive the gift of the Spirit in confirmation by simply opening ourselves to the work of the Spirit in us. As St Paul says:

> 'When the kindness and love of God our saviour for mankind were revealed, it was not because he was concerned with any righteous actions we might have done ourselves: it was for no reason except for his own compassion that he saved us, by means of the cleansing water of rebirth and by renewing us with the Holy Spirit which he has so generously poured over us through Jesus Christ our saviour.' (*Titus 3:4-7*)

During this confirmation programme the group can sometimes pause to sum up its growth in the Spirit through the celebration of the Eucharistic Liturgy. It would be good to begin the programme by a votive Mass of the Holy Spirit. Ideally, this could be celebrated in the parish church, with the parish priest presiding, and the parishioners invited.

Before embarking on a session decide what human experience the group will live together. Plan the experience so that all can benefit from it. When you come together for the specific prayer session recall that experience and use it to lead the group into the spiritual dimension, following the progression explained in **MAKING THE SESSION WORK** (pp. 15ff).

The sessions have been divided into three parts.

Part I *Building the Community* has fourteen sessions. In session seven, New Life Together, each mentally handicapped person will be presented with a Good News Bible. The giving of the Book of God's Word to each mentally handicapped person signifies the importance of the Word of God for the community. This little Christian community has come together over a period of time to listen to and to speak the words of Jesus to one another. The receiving of the Book of Good News by the handicapped person will be a sign for him that he too is a friend of Jesus and that he will listen attentively to the words of Jesus.

Part II *Waiting for the Spirit* is the immediate preparation for confirmation and has thirteen sessions.

Part III *Filled with the Spirit* is a more practical section. As you get to know your group and especially each individual handicapped person you will discover his gifts. These gifts can then become the basis for helping the handicapped person to carry out a ministry within the local community.

Liturgies in the parish could from time to time include prayers of thanksgiving for the different gifts and ministries of the people of God. This would enable the handicapped person to belong to the parish in a concrete way and to carry out his mission to serve. For this reason only two sample sessions are given in this section.

The Prayer Group or Catechetical Group will continue to be the context for ongoing spiritual formation where all the activities, social or spiritual, are brought together and offered to the Lord and to one another. It is hoped that when you get this far in the programme your little community will reflect some if not all of the characteristics of the early Christian community:

> The faithful all met together. They went as a body to
> the Temple but met in their homes for the breaking of
> bread. *(Acts of the Apostles 2:45-47)*

Provision has been made for eucharistic liturgies and a paraliturgy on wholeness. The eucharist binds the community together in Christ and enables its members to witness to the world their spirit-filled life of praise. Except for the confirmation liturgy themes have only been suggested. It seems better and more appropriate to allow the groups to work out their own eucharistic celebration. Much of the preparation needed for these celebrations can be done by the group especially if the liturgy is held in the usual meeting place. The group can, for example, prepare its own bread, water, wine and vestments. The chalice can be polished and the candles trimmed and cleaned, Activities such as these draw people into the event and allow for greater participation in the actual celebration of Mass.

May you be filled with the Holy Spirit and continue to pray and to serve in the company of your mentally handicapped brothers and sisters for the building up of the Kingdom.

Part I

BUILDING THE COMMUNITY

AIM
To help each person to feel welcome and to welcome others.
This attitude of openness in welcome is the first movement in
worship.

HUMAN EXPERIENCE
*The actual welcome into the group for each individual
person.*

SPIRITUAL DIMENSION

PREPARATION
For this session you will need:
—the Book of God's Word;
—a candle;
—some fresh flowers;
—appropriate music;
—a large key concealed in a box.

RECALL THE HUMAN EXPERIENCE
It is good to see you all.
It's so good to see you, John.
I am happy you could come.
Name each one slowly.
What have we got here, I wonder?
It's a nice box.
I wonder if there is something inside the box?
Pick up the box—shake it.
Yes, something is making a heavy thud.
Let's open the box.
Do so very carefully and slowly.
Create anticipation.
It's a key, a very big key.
Take the key to each one to see.
Encourage comments.
*Make sure each person knows how a key fits in the
lock of a door.*

When the door is locked and someone knocks...
Knock hard on some object.
...I go to the door.
I turn the key and the door knob and the door opens.
I say 'Come in!'
I'm happy to welcome a friend.
Tonight I knew that all of you were coming to our group.
I wanted to welcome you all.
I wanted to welcome you, John.
Mention each one by name.
So I got here early, and I unlocked all the doors.
Mime.
I opened all the doors wide.
Gesture.
You all came. You are all here.
Name each one again. Don't forget the helpers!
I am so happy to see you all.
We can all be friends together.
We can all be friends, especially John and Michael.
Mention each handicapped person in relation to his/her friend (Catechist).
We are all friends together.

DEEPEN THE HUMAN EXPERIENCE
We are together now.
John and Michael are here with us all.
Name each handicapped person and helper in the same way.
We are happy together.
It's good to be together.
We welcomed one another tonight.

CHURCH DIMENSION
We welcomed one another to our Mass with Father... last week.
Mention place and priest of your opening Mass.
We welcomed Father... too, didn't we?

We were happy with the priest.
You were happy with the priest, John.
   Address each one.
We all stood up when the priest came in to say Mass.
We welcomed him.
The priest welcomed us.
He said, 'Welcome! Welcome to John! Welcome to Mary!'
   Name each one or group.
He said welcome to our families.
We were happy.
We sang together.
We sang 'Walk in the light'.
   Choose a hymn from your opening liturgy to sing.

PROCLAIM THE GOOD NEWS
   At Mass we listened to Father…
We listened to Jesus.
   Pause.
Tonight we listen to Jesus in the Holy Book.
   Pause.
   Stand up, move slowly and deliberately towards the Holy Book.
   Pick it up reverently.
   Raise it up for all to see.
   Extend it towards the group.
In the Holy Book Jesus speaks to us:
   'Look, I am standing at your door knocking.
   If you hear me calling and open the door,
   I will come in.'   *Revelation 3:20*
   Repeat three times, at least.
   Slowly put the book back.
   Face the group.
We are all friends.
We want to become very good friends.
We want Jesus to be with us.
   Gesture.

Go to each person, taking their hands.

John, Jesus says to you tonight:
   'I am with you.'
   When you have given the message to each one,
   face the group again.
Jesus says to all of us tonight:
   'I am with you.'
   Pause.

RESPONDING TO THE MESSAGE

Choose a suitable piece of music to help the group
assimilate the message and to give them the
opportunity to respond.
I suggest you listen together to
♪   *'Rat-a-tat-tat. Oh, who is that?*
      It's Jesus knocking on your door.'
from the album 'Rainbow' (Anchor Recordings).
Play it again so that people can join in.
Find an appropriate way to bring the session to
a close and to end the evening together.

Part I Session 2
FRIENDS

AIM

To be aware that we are happy when we are together as
friends. When we are together like this, Jesus is with us.

HUMAN EXPERIENCE

Being friends together. Doing things that create unity,
interaction and deepen friendship within the group.
It is important that the meeting place is carefully prepared
and that people are warmly welcomed without being
fussed over or talked to in a condescending manner.
Introduce people to one another. Give enough time for
each person to adjust to the room and to the other people.

SPIRITUAL DIMENSION

PREPARATION

For this session you will need:
—the Book of God's Word;
—a candle;
—some fresh flowers;
—something concrete to help the group focus on
friendship, for example, photographs;
—appropriate music.

RECALL THE HUMAN EXPERIENCE

John, I am happy that you are here tonight.
Tom, I am happy that you are here tonight.
Mary, I am happy that you are here tonight.

Address each person in the group individually by
name, handicapped and non-handicapped.

I want you to be happy here.
I want this place to be our special place.
I enjoyed preparing it for you, John.
I enjoyed preparing it for you, Tom.

Name each one as before.
Mention special things you did to get the place
ready.

Joan, when you came here last time you met Susan,
<u>your</u> special friend.
Tom, <u>you</u> met your special friend too, didn't you?
John is your special friend.

Mention each person and their special friend,
and help them to begin to relate to one another.

You are happy together Mary and Tina.

Involve everyone by naming them in a similar way.

I have a photograph of you, Mary.
Look! There is Tina.
You are enjoying yourselves!

Show photographs of the group doing something
together.

We are all enjoying ourselves.
We may have been a little afraid

wondering what would happen to us
and who we were going to meet.
Now we feel better.
We have friends here.
You have many friends here, Joan.
Address each person in the same way.

DEEPEN THE HUMAN EXPERIENCE

<u>We</u> are all friends.
When we meet new friends,
people who say 'Hello, how are you?',
people who welcome us,
people who like us,
we are happy, we are very happy.
We feel good.
We want to be together.
We are happy to be together.

CHURCH DIMENSION

When we are together
Jesus is with us.
When we are happy to be together
Jesus is with us.
When we come here around the Holy Book
Jesus is with us.
When we read from the Holy Book
Jesus speaks to us.
Jesus is with us.

PROCLAIM THE GOOD NEWS

Moment of silence.
This can be enhanced by quiet reflective music
during which you pick up the Bible reverently
and solemnly.
In the Holy Book Jesus says:
'Where two or three meet in my name,
I shall be there with them.'   *Matthew 18:20*
Repeat once.
Jesus says:
'When you are together,
I am with you.'

THE MESSAGE

> *Go to each one,*
> *call each one by name,*
> *take their hands and say:*
> John, Jesus says to you tonight:
>   'I am with you.'
> *When you have spoken to everyone individually,*
> *address the whole group.*
> Jesus says to all of us tonight:
>   'I am with you.'

RESPONDING TO THE MESSAGE

> *Choose a suitable piece of music that will help each*
> *person to understand better that 'Jesus is with me'*
> *and to give them the opportunity to respond.*

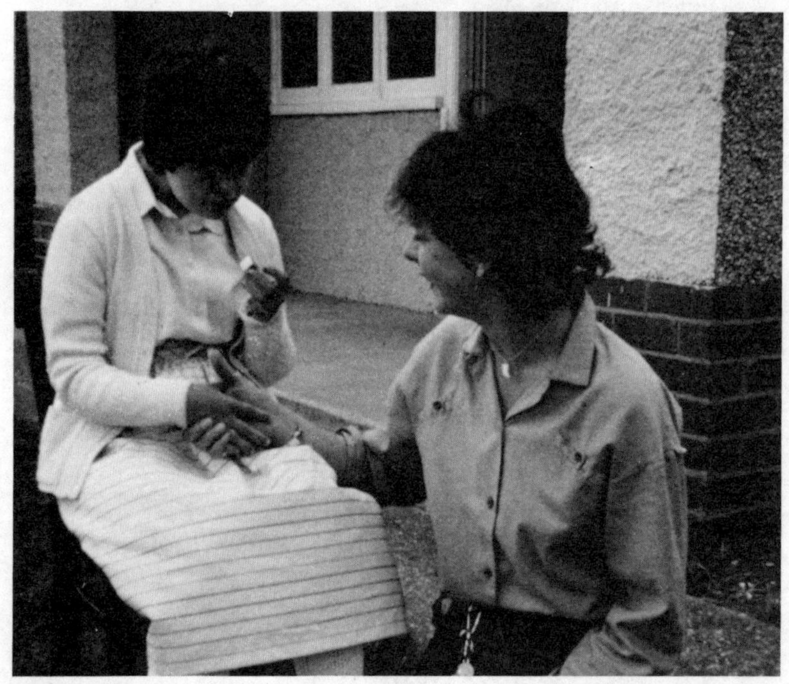

Friends together.

AIM

To become aware that as a group of friends we experience the spirit of peace and joy. Jesus calls us to love one another so that we can know the spirit of love.

HUMAN EXPERIENCE

Being together as a group.
Meeting in the special place.
Welcoming one another.
Sharing together

SPIRITUAL DIMENSION

PREPARATION

Prepare your special place with:
—the Book of God's Word;
—a candle;
—fresh flowers.
You will also need:
—appropriate music.

RECALL THE HUMAN EXPERIENCE

I look forward to Monday evenings.

Or whichever is appropriate.

I look forward to seeing all my friends again.

I look forward to you coming, Mary.

Name each person.

I come early to get the place ready.

I like to have the place ready for each one of you.

I get the place ready for Tom and Betty.

I get the place ready for John and Simon.

Name each one in relation to their friend,
and what they like to do together.

I like to be here waiting for you, John.

I like to be here waiting for you, Joan.

Address each one individually.

John is always here early.
I'm happy to see you, John.
Then Mary and Tom and Miss Smith come.
> *Name the arrival of people and the usual ritual.*
How good it is to see you all again.
It's good to be here all together.
How good it is to have everybody together.

DEEPEN THE HUMAN EXPERIENCE

When we come together here we get to know one
another better.
We are becoming good friends.
We welcome one another.
We're glad to be together.
We share together.
We have fun together.
> *Elaborate as appropriate.*
We help one another.
We are happy together.
We like being together.

CHURCH DIMENSION

I think we need one another. Don't you?
> *Name all the things for which you need one
> another.*
We need all our friends.
We need one another to be happy.
When we are together Jesus is with us.
We need Jesus.
We need the Spirit of Jesus to be with us.
The Spirit of Jesus is with us when we come
together here.
When we are happy together with others
the Spirit of Jesus is with us.

PROCLAIM THE GOOD NEWS

In the Holy Book Jesus says:
> 'I give you a new commandment:
> Love one another.

Just as I have loved you,
you also must love one another.'   *John 13:34-35*

THE MESSAGE
> *Go to each person,*
> *call them by name and say:*
> John, Jesus says to you tonight:
> 'I love you.
> Love one another.'
> *Then address the whole group:*
> Jesus says to all of us tonight:
> 'I love you.
> Love one another.'

RESPONDING TO THE MESSAGE
> *Choose a song which will help to sum up the group's joy at being together listening to the Good News and which will be a fitting conclusion to the session.*

Part I Session 4
CALLED TO BE FRIENDS

AIM
To become aware of the call to belong to the group and of the call to new life which Jesus addresses to each of us.

HUMAN EXPERIENCE
> *Plan something specific as a group.*
> *This could be an outing or a 'get-together' party to celebrate your friendship.*

SPIRITUAL DIMENSION

PREPARATION

Prepare your special place with:
—the Book of God's Word;
—a candle;
—fresh flowers.
You will also need:
—appropriate music.

RECALL THE HUMAN EXPERIENCE

It is good to be together again.
> *Help each one to express as best as they are able*
> *what being together means to them.*

Because we are friends we celebrate.
We had a great outing or party.
> *Talk about what you did.*

We belong together as friends.
We celebrate our belonging.
It is so good to be with you, Tom.
> *Address each one individually.*
> *Help and encourage them to express their joy at*
> *belonging.*

I am happy to belong.
I am happy to belong with each one of you.
I am happy to be called to belong to this group.
You are happy, Tom. You are happy to belong.
> *Encourage sharing if this is possible.*

To be with you makes us happy.
To be with you gives me courage.
To be with friends gives us courage.

DEEPEN THE HUMAN EXPERIENCE

When we belong together we feel strong.
When we belong together we have courage.
When I am with you I feel courage to do lots of things.
> *Name various things the group enable you to do.*

You have courage because you belong, John.
You feel better.

You feel strong.
You are not afraid to try out new jobs.
*Address each one
and name something specific that he can do
because of the encouragement of the group.*
We are full of courage when we belong together.
We have courage when we are called to belong.

CHURCH DIMENSION

When we come together here we feel strong.
Here together around the Holy Book we feel
encouraged.
We listen to the promises of Jesus.
This gives us courage.
Jesus calls us to belong together.
Jesus calls us to belong to him.
We respond to the call of Jesus.
We are given courage.

PROCLAIM THE GOOD NEWS

In the Holy Book we read:
'Do not be afraid…
I have called you by your name,
you are mine.
…Do not be afraid,
for I am with you.'   *Isaiah 43:1*

THE MESSAGE

*Go to each person,
call them by name and say:*
John, Jesus says to you tonight:
'I am with you.'
Then address the whole group:
Jesus says to all of us tonight:
'I am with you.'

Choose a piece of music or a song that will help to give the sense of joy and hope that should come from knowing 'Jesus is with us.' For example,
♪ *'Jesus is with us' from the album 'Good morning, Jesus.' (Palm Tree Records).*

Climbing.

Part I Session 5
CALLED BY NAME

AIM

To help each person become aware that each is unique.
To relate to God as I really am in the name of Jesus through the Spirit gives glory to God.

HUMAN EXPERIENCE

*Looking at a bunch of beautiful flowers mainly of one kind,
but among which there is one different.*
*Recognising that it is different, but that it, too, is
beautiful.*
*(The human experience and its spiritual dimension can be
incorporated into one in this session.)*

SPIRITUAL DIMENSION

PREPARATION

Prepare your special place with:
—the Book of God's Word;
—a candle.
You will also need:
—a bunch of flowers of one kind (e.g. daffodils);
*—one single flower among that bunch that
  is noticeably different (e.g. a rose);*
—a large vase in which you put all the flowers;
*—a smaller vase you will use later for the 'different'
  flower;*
—appropriate music.

RECALL THE HUMAN EXPERIENCE

I brought you some flowers tonight.
Aren't they lovely?
They smell good too.
They are sunshine colour.
I feel good when I see these flowers.
*Smell the flowers,
and show that you enjoy doing it.
Invite everyone else to do the same,
as you bring the flowers to them.
Talk about the flowers.
Name them.
Help everyone to notice that one of the flowers
is different.*
This is different.
This is a rose.

All the others are daffodils.
The rose smells good doesn't it, John?
Let people handle and smell the rose.
Allow plenty of time.
The rose is a very special flower.
It is beautiful.
I am going to put one rose into this little vase.
There! Isn't that lovely!
Now the rose is in water.
The water will keep it fresh for some time.
Can you smell the lovely scent?
The scent fills the room.
Describe the rose to the group.
The rose is different from the daffodils.
The rose is beautiful.
Pause.
I am different, too.
I am different from other people.
I'm glad I'm different.
I'm glad I'm *me*.
I'm your friend.
John is different from Michael.
John is John, Michael is Michael.
Mention each one individually.
I'm glad John is John.
I'm glad Michael is Michael.
Address each one in a similar way.
John is my friend.
I am John's friend.
Address each one individually.

DEEPEN THE HUMAN EXPERIENCE
I am glad I am me.
I am glad John is John.
I am glad Mary is Mary.
Mention each one and allow time for responses.
We are all friends just as we are.
We are good friends.

We are good friends together here in our special place.
Name each one.
We are good friends
here around the Holy Book.
We are good friends
when we meet around the altar
at Mass.
When we go to Mass Father David calls us by name.
Father David says 'Welcome, John!'
He calls John
by name.
Father David says 'Welcome, Mary!'
He calls Mary
by name.
Mention each one individually.
We are called by name.
John is called by name.
Mary is called by name.
Mention each one individually.
We are happy.
Pause.

PROCLAIM THE GOOD NEWS

We are happy to be together.
When we are together like this Jesus is with us.
We prepare our hearts to listen to Jesus.
We light our candle.
We are still for a moment.
We listen.
Go slowly towards the Holy Book.
Pick it up reverently and say:
In the Holy Book Jesus says:
'Think of all the flowers in the fields.
You are of much more value than any of them.
Your heavenly Father knows what you need.
He knows you by your name.
I have called you by name.
You are mine.'   *Matthew 6:26-33 & Isaiah 43:1*

Jesus says to you today:
'My Father calls you by your name, John.'
Address each person individually.

RESPONDING TO THE MESSAGE

♪ *'I heard the Lord call my name.'*
Songs of the Spirit, no. 30;
Hymns Old & New, no. 118;
Hymns Old & New Enlarged, no. 237.

Part I Session 6
CALLED TO BE ONE FAMILY

AIM

To become aware that we belong to one family—God's family.
Through our baptism we are called to share in his life and love.

HUMAN EXPERIENCE

Sharing in a celebration of baptism, or, if this is not
possible, viewing a video or slides of a baptism.

SPIRITUAL DIMENSION

PREPARATION

Prepare your special place with:
—the Book of God's Word;
—a candle;
—fresh flowers.
You will also need:
—equipment for the video or slides;
—appropriate music.

RECALL THE HUMAN EXPERIENCE

If you were at the baptism, recall the experience in

a way that will help the handicapped person.
If not, use the following progression.
I have something very special to show you today.
As you show slides or begin video.
These people came together for something special.
This is...
Name the person.
Here are some more of our friends.
Mention people by name.
They are here at the church to celebrate.
They are celebrating that someone new has come into
their family.
Look who it is!
Give time for handicapped person to react.
Yes, it is their new baby.
Tom and Mary (or Mr and Mrs Houlihan)
brought their baby daughter to the church
so that she could come into God's family.
Here is Father David.
He welcomes all the family.
He is admiring the baby.
Here they all are gathered round the priest.
The priest prays and pours holy water over the
baby's head.
The priest baptises the baby.
He asks Mrs Houlihan the baby's name.
He says:
    'I baptise you, Clare,
    in the name of the Father,
    and of the Son,
    and of the Holy Spirit.'
Now the baby belongs to God's family.
Baby Clare comes into God's family at baptism.
Everyone is happy.
Look at Mum and Dad smiling.
They are happy.
Mention the joy and happiness of the group.
Everybody is happy .
because baby Clare belongs to God's family.

DEEPEN THE HUMAN EXPERIENCE

We belong to God's family.
John, you belong to God's family.
Name each handicapped person and each catechist.
We all belong to God's family.
We all belong together in God's house.
We all belong to God's family.
John's Mum took him to church to belong to God's family.
The priest prayed and poured holy water over John's head.
The priest said:
'I baptise you, John,
in the name of the Father,
and of the Son,
and of the Holy Spirit.'
Shane's Mum took him to church to belong to God's family.
Repeat the procedure until all 'know'
they belong to God's family through baptism.
We all belong together in God's family
with Jesus and the Holy Spirit.

CHURCH DIMENSION

Here together around the Holy Book we belong to God's family.
When we are together like this Jesus is with us.
We prepare our hearts.
We light our candle.
We listen to God's Word—Jesus.

PROCLAIM THE GOOD NEWS

In the Holy Book Jesus tells his friends to help
people to belong to God's family.
Jesus says:
'Go and gather together all my friends;
baptise them in the name of the Father
and of the Son
and of the Holy Spirit
and they will belong to my Father's family.'
Matthew 28:19-20

THE MESSAGE

> *Go to each one, call them by name, and say:*
> John, Jesus says to you today:
> 'You belong to the family of God.'

RESPONDING TO THE MESSAGE

> *Sing a song that will help to reinforce the message*
> *of 'belonging to God', and give everyone a chance to*
> *express it: for example,*
> ♪ *'Belonging'*
> *from 'We celebrate the Eucharist.' (Silver Burdett).*

Part I Session 7
NEW LIFE TOGETHER

AIM

To become aware that we belong to a group, a community,
as friends of God listening to the words of Jesus. Each one will
belong to the extent that he or she feels called, welcomed,
chosen.

During this session the Good News Bible will be presented to
each mentally handicapped person as a sign that he will live as
a friend of God and that he will listen to the words of Jesus.

HUMAN EXPERIENCE

> *Collecting beautiful stones or admiring a friend's*
> *collection.*

SPIRITUAL DIMENSION

PREPARATION

> *You will need:*
> *—the Book of God's Word;*
> *—a large candle;*
> *—a large glass bowl with water in it;*
> *—a collection of brightly coloured stones in a basket;*
> *—one copy of the 'Good News Bible' for each*
> *   handicapped person;*
> *—appropriate music.*

We had a great time on Saturday.
It was good to be with you all.
It was great to see you, John.
Mention each person in a similar way.
It was fun being together, wasn't it?
We went to collect our beautiful stones.
or
We went to see Mark's lovely collection.
Use whatever is most appropriate for your group.
Here they are in the basket.
Allow time for people to focus and to admire the collection.
They are all so lovely.
Which stone would you like, Mary?
This one or this one?
Give the person time to choose.
Yes, that is a beautiful stone, Mary.
Repeat with the other members of the group.
Then take one yourself.
I think I would like to put my stone into this bowl of water.
Go slowly to bowl and put the stone in.
See, it's going down.
See, how it shines in the water.
Give time for people to focus and to react.
Invite people to put their stones in too.
John, would you like to put your stone in the water?
There it goes.
How lovely!
Repeat with each one.
If someone does not want to put their stone in,
talk about it being beautiful in the water some day.
This person may put the stone in towards the end
of the session.
Invite each one to put the stone in.
Invite each one to make a contribution to the group.
Look at your stone, Mary.
It is so beautiful in the water.

Your stone is really pretty, Margaret.
Help each one to identify with their stones in the water.
Our stones look so beautiful <u>together</u>.
I want to see them all <u>together</u> in the light.
*Light the candle
and position it so that the bowl catches a reflection.*
Oh!
Be still and allow time for the group to experience a sense of wonder and awe.

DEEPEN THE HUMAN EXPERIENCE

We are all together.
Name each person.
We are all together around the water.
Gesture.
We are all together in the light.
Gesture.
That makes me so happy.
You are happy John aren't you?
Address each person quietly.
We are happy together.
We belong together.
We belong together in the light.
Mention each one individually.
We are happy to be together.
We are happy to be together in the light.
We belong in the light.

CHURCH DIMENSION

We are gathered together in the light.
We are gathered together in the light around the Holy Book.
Mention each person present individually.
We are gathered together to listen to the Word of God.
The Word of God is light.
I want to speak the words of Jesus to you, John.
I want to speak the words of Jesus to you, Mary.

Mention each one.
We love Jesus.
He is important in our lives.
Solemnly call each one by name and say:
John, you are a friend of God.
You will listen to Jesus.
I give you the book of Good News.
Do the same for each person.
After a moment of silence, introduce an
appropriate song:
for example, the refrain
♪   *'Alleluia. Praise the Lord'*
from the song 'Thank you, Lord.' on the Carey
Landry album 'Hi God!' (NALR).

PROCLAIM THE GOOD NEWS

In the Holy Book, a friend of Jesus tells us:
    'Brothers and Sisters,
    you have been called.
    You are chosen.
    You will belong to the Kingdom
    of our Lord and Saviour, Jesus Christ.
    You love me—keep my words...'   *2 Peter 1:10-11*

THE MESSAGE

Go to each one, call them by name, and say:
Jesus says to you today:
    I <u>chose</u> you to belong.
    Listen to me.

RESPONDING TO THE MESSAGE

Use music and song appropriate to the session.
Perhaps you could share a simple meal together to
emphasise the sense of belonging together.

AIM

To become aware of the fullness of life that is ours when we choose to live in God's way. Jesus brings life now and promises us its fullness in the Kingdom of God.

HUMAN EXPERIENCE

Planting bulbs, sowing flower seeds or, if possible, gardening. Watching the plants grow.

SPIRITUAL DIMENSION

PREPARATION

You will need:
—the Book of God's Word;
—a candle;
—your plants;
—appropriate music.

RECALL THE HUMAN EXPERIENCE

Our plants are really growing, aren't they?
Look at John's, it's really healthy,
and Mary's is shooting up too.
> *Think about the care given to the plants by the group.*
This is my favourite plant.
> *Take one plant and build the session around it.*
We had this plant on the window sill.
We knew it would need light and air.
It needs light and air to grow.
Did you notice how it grew towards the light?
> *Address each person,*
> *commenting on the plant growing towards the light.*
It likes the sun.
We made sure it got plenty of sun, plenty of light.
Tom, you moved it into the light didn't you?
It reaches towards the light.

Use gesture if this will help emphasis reaching
upwards.

The leaves are very healthy and it's growing very fast.
It has become more beautiful.
It is strong and healthy.
It keeps reaching towards the light.
It is full of life.

DEEPEN THE HUMAN EXPERIENCE

We have life too.
We choose to grow.
We choose life.
We choose to be in the light too.
Pause.
Move the plant out of the light.

Sometimes we don't grow as we could.
We don't love as we could.
We turn away.
We are unhappy.
Pause.

But we really do want to grow.
We want to love.
We choose to grow so we say 'I'm sorry'.
Then we turn again towards the light.
Move the plant back into the light.

We choose the light.
We are happy again.
We are full of love.
We are in the light.
Pause.

We want to grow in the light.

CHURCH DIMENSION

Here together around the Holy Book
we receive life.
We listen to God's Word.
We want to choose life.
We want to grow in the light of God.
We are filled with life.
We are happy.

Together we rejoice in God's word of life.
Sometimes we sing and praise God.
We sing...
> *Sing a hymn of praise familiar to the group.*

PROCLAIM THE GOOD NEWS
> Jesus brings life.
> In the Holy Book, Jesus says:
>> I have come
>> that you may have life
>> and have it to the full.   *John 10:10*

THE MESSAGE
>> *Go to each person individually,*
>> *call them by name and say:*
> John, Jesus says to you today / tonight:
>> I give you life,
>> my life in you.
>> *Then address the whole group:*
> Jesus says to all of us today / tonight:
>> I give you life,
>> my life in you.

RESPONDING TO THE MESSAGE
> *Choose a suitable hymn through which to express*
> *together praise and thanks to God for the fullness*
> *of life that is ours.*

Part I Session 9
CELEBRATING LIFE

AIM
To celebrate our being together as a community
and especially to celebrate our friend's birthday.
**This session can be used for a birthday or an anniversary*
celebration in the group.

HUMAN EXPERIENCE

*A birthday or an anniversary party
or welcoming people back after an absence.*

SPIRITUAL DIMENSION

RECALL THE HUMAN EXPERIENCE

How good it is to see you all again.
It's good to see you, Rita.
We missed you last time.
And you, Guy, we missed you, too.
Did you have a good holiday?
It's good to see you…
*Name each one individually.
Pause.*
We are all together again.
We are all together in the light.
We are all together round the Holy Book.
I am so happy.
…is with us around the Holy Book in the light.
Mention each one individually.
We are all together.
We are happy to be together.
We are happy to be together on Ron's birthday.
We celebrate with Ron.
We celebrate his birthday.
We sing Happy Birthday.

CHURCH DIMENSION

We are happy to celebrate Ron's birthday.
Whenever we share in a birthday party
we are full of joy. Our hearts are full of joy.
We celebrate life.
When we are together like this Jesus is with us.
Jesus is with us as we come together around the
Holy Book.
Our hearts are full of joy.
Sing together (or listen to) the song
♪   *'I've got joy! joy! joy!'*
from the Carey Landry album 'Hi God!' (NALR).

In the Holy Book Jesus says:
'When two or three are gathered in my name,
I am with you.   *Matthew 18:20*
People will know that you are my friend
by the love you show to one another.'   *John 13:35*
Repeat.

THE MESSAGE

Go to each person and address them individually:
…Jesus says to you today/tonight:
'You are my friend.
I love you.'
*When you have spoken to everyone individually,
turn to the group again:*
Jesus says to all of us:
'I love you.'

RESPONDING TO THE MESSAGE

Let's show that we love one another.
Let's give a sign of peace to one another.
*While you all exchange the sign of peace,
let there be some appropriate music.
For example, sing (or play)
♪   'Peacetime.'
Folk Hymnal Volume 4, no 37;
Carey Landry album 'Hi God!' (NALR).
Let this song draw the more explicitly spiritual
part of the session to a close—but hopefully the
birthday or anniversary celebration will now follow.*

Part I Session 10
FRIENDS TOGETHER IN FORGIVENESS

AIM

To become aware of the joy of being forgiven. God binds us
together in love.

HUMAN EXPERIENCE
Something that caused upset to one person in the group or something that one person omitted to do that causes unhappiness in the group.

SPIRITUAL DIMENSION

PREPARATION
For this session you will need:
—the Book of God's Word;
—fresh flowers;
—appropriate music;
—a candle, which for this session only,
should be lit for the Proclamation of the Good News.

RECALL THE HUMAN EXPERIENCE
We (*or* Tom) had a hard time last week.
We are happy now.
We are glad to be together again.
Get the group to talk about the unhappiness.
Did you ever feel that everyone was mad with you?
I did.
Mention occasions and what you did.
Get other members of the group to do likewise.
When I said 'I'm sorry' everything was all right.
I was happy again.
My friend (*or* friends) forgave me.
It was all right again.
I was so happy.
Get people to focus on the desire to be _at_ peace with one another.
Encourage those who can to share their experiences.
When we say we are sorry we hope the other person will forgive us.
When we are forgiven we are happy again.
We have peace.
We are friends again.
We learn to be more careful next time.

DEEPEN THE HUMAN EXPERIENCE

It is good to be friends.
It is good to say 'I'm sorry'.
It is good to be forgiven.
It is good to be at peace with one another.
We are all happy together again.

CHURCH DIMENSION

When we pray
we tell God we are sorry too.
We ask God to help us to be better,
to love one another.
We know God hears us.
When we go to Mass we tell God we are sorry
all together with the priest.
We say, 'I confess'.
We say, 'Lord, have mercy.
Christ, have mercy.
Lord, have mercy.'
We all think about how we have hurt our friends
and other people.
We think of how we have offended God our Father.
Everyone says '*We* are sorry.'
In the name of God the priest says:
'<u>You</u> are forgiven.'
Then everyone is happy again.
We share the Sign of Peace.
Give each other the Sign of Peace.

PROCLAIM THE GOOD NEWS

Light the candle, and pick up the Holy Book with reverence.
In the Holy Book, Jesus says:
'Your sins are forgiven.
You are forgiven.'   *Luke 7:48*
Repeat as often as seems appropriate.

> *Go to each person, take their hands and say:*
> Tom, are you sorry for not loving others?
> *Allow time for each person to nod or to say 'Yes'.*
> Jesus says to you tonight:
> *Place your hands on the person's head.*
> Your sins are forgiven.
> You are forgiven.
> Jesus says to all of us here tonight:
> Your sins are forgiven.
> You are forgiven.

RESPONDING TO THE MESSAGE

> *Sing a song together through which the group can*
> *express the joy of forgiveness, for example,*
> ♪ *'Freely, freely'*
> *Songs of the Spirit, no. 12;*
> *Hymns Old & New, no. 84;*
> *Hymns Old & New Enlarged, no. 175.*

Part I Session 11
WE BELONG TOGETHER

AIM

To become aware of our belonging together. The spirit of Jesus unites us in love as we grow together.

HUMAN EXPERIENCE

> *Emphasise the group spirit and how you have grown*
> *together.*
> *Perhaps you could have a special meal together to*
> *celebrate your belonging.*

SPIRITUAL DIMENSION

PREPARATION

> *For this session you will need:*
> *—the Book of God's Word;*

—a candle;
—fresh flowers;
—appropriate music.

RECALL THE HUMAN EXPERIENCE

I am really glad that I met John.
It's good to know you, John, and you, Mary.
I am happy to be with you.
  Mention each member of the group in a similar way.
I am happy that we are all here together.
  Ask the members of the group how they feel.
We belong together.
We get on well together.
We like being together.
We do so many things together.
  Name some of the things you do.
We share together.
We pray together.
Each one gives of himself.
  Mention the specific quality or gift each
  individual brings to the group.
John, you bring something special to our group
when you smile.
John, I feel so good.
Don't we all?
  Turning to the whole group again.
Each of us shares.
Each one of us helps the group to grow strong.
Each one helps to make the group happy.
We are happy together.
We are <u>one</u> together. We are one in the Spirit.
  Sing chorus of
  ♪ *'We are one in the Spirit.'*
  20th Century Folk Hymnal Volume 1, no. 46.
We belong together.
All of us belong together.
Tom belongs to us.
  Name each person in the same way.
We all belong together in this group.

DEEPEN THE HUMAN EXPERIENCE

To be <u>one</u> together—that is good.
To be one in the Spirit makes me very happy.
This makes you happy, Mary; and you, Susan.
Address each member of the group in the same way.
I know we are one.
I am so thankful,
I give thanks to God.
Pause.

CHURCH DIMENSION

When we gather together here around the Holy Book
we offer thanks to God.
When we go to Mass,
when we gather near the altar with Father...
Name the priest familiar with the group.
we offer ourselves.
We offer all that we have to the Lord.
The Lord receives our gifts.
The Lord fills us with his Spirit.
His Spirit fills us with love and joy.
His Spirit joins us together.

PROCLAIM THE GOOD NEWS

In the Holy Book, Jesus says:
'My Spirit lives in you.'   *John 14:16-17*

THE MESSAGE

Go to each person, call them by name and say:
Tom, Jesus says to you tonight:
'My Spirit lives in you.'
Turn to the whole group:
Jesus says to all of us here tonight:
'My Spirit lives in you.'

RESPONDING TO THE MESSAGE

*Choose an appropriate song or piece of music to
express joy and thanksgiving for sharing the one
Spirit of God.*

Conkers.

Part I Session 12
FRIENDS GIVE PRAISE

AIM

To give praise and thanks to God through Jesus for the beauty
we see around us.

HUMAN EXPERIENCE

*A trip to a park or into the country to see the beauty of the
flowers, the shrubs and the trees.*

SPIRITUAL DIMENSION

PREPARATION

For this session you will need:
—the Book of God's Word;
—a candle;
—fresh flowers;
—slides/photographs of the trip to see the flowers
  (or slides/photographs of flowers);
—appropriate music.

RECALL THE HUMAN EXPERIENCE

What a wonderful trip we had last...
  Name day.
I took some slides (photographs) for us to keep as
souvenirs.
Look at this.
These are the...
  Name flowers.
  Go through the slides slowly.
  Allow everyone the time to relive the wonder of
  seeing such beauty.

DEEPEN THE HUMAN EXPERIENCE

When I see such beauty I am happy.
When you see the beautiful flowers,
you are happy, Mary.
  Address each person.
When I see the blue sky and feel the warm sun
I am happy.
When the sky is blue and the sun is shining and warm,
you are happy, Tom.
  Address each person.
I am happy to be alive.
It is good to smell the new cut grass.
It's great to hear the birds singing.
You feel good too, John.
  Address each one.

I am happy to be able to enjoy all that beauty
with my friends,
with all of you, my special friends.
I am full of joy.
I am really happy.
I am glad to be alive.
I am glad that I am Maggie.
I am happy to be alive.
You are full of joy, Joan.
I know you are.
You are happy to be alive.
> *Address each person and help each one identify
> with the beauty of life.*

CHURCH DIMENSION

When we come together here
we are happy to be alive.
When we come together here around the Holy Book
we are happy to be alive.
Sometimes we sing and dance with joy.
We praise God through Jesus.
Let us sing a song of praise together.
> *An appropriate song, for example:*
> ♪   *'Praise him, praise him.'*
> *Folk Hymnal Volume 2, no. 60;*
> *Hymns Old & New, no. 222;*
> *Hymns Old & New Enlarged, no. 448.*

PROCLAIM THE GOOD NEWS

In the Holy Book we read how the people of God
prayed.
They praised God like this:
> 'O Lord our God, how great you are.'   *Psalm 8*
> *Repeat.*

THE MESSAGE

> *Go to each one, call them by name and say:*
John, Jesus asks you to pray with him tonight:

'O Lord our God, how great you are.'
Use an appropriate gesture.
Address the whole group:
Jesus asks us all to pray with him tonight:
'O Lord our God, how great you are.'
Again, use gesture.

RESPONDING TO THE MESSAGE
A song of praise and thanksgiving.

A picnic during an outing.

Part I Session 13
STRENGTH IN FRIENDSHIP

AIM

To become aware that friends help us to be strong. That strength comes from the presence of friends. That the believing community longs for the strengthening Spirit which leads to a firmer commitment to life.

HUMAN EXPERIENCE
The friendship which has grown between individuals and among the group as a whole.

SPIRITUAL DIMENSION

PREPARATION

For this session you will need:
—the Book of God's Word;
—a candle;
—fresh flowers;
—appropriate music.

RECALL THE HUMAN EXPERIENCE

We really are happy to come together.
I watched you welcome one another tonight
and what a joy!
I wish I could recapture what happened
when each of you welcomed the other.
I wonder how you felt.
You felt good, didn't you, John?
And so did you, Mary.
>   *Address each person and encourage participation.*

We certainly are friends.
There's no doubt about that.
We feel the power of friendship.
We are good friends.
>   *Pause.*

A good friend helps me to be strong.
A good friend helps me not to be afraid.
A good friend helps me to reach out to others,
to be with others.
>   *Pause.*

Tom has a good friend—Tony.
Tony has a good friend—Tom.
>   *Name each person in relation to their friend.*

DEEPEN THE HUMAN EXPERIENCE

We are all friends.
We want to be together.
We want to help one another to be strong.
To be full of love for other people.
When we are together we feel the power of our
friendship.
This gives us such joy.

CHURCH DIMENSION

When we come here around the Holy Book
we welcome the Word of God.
We love one another.
We feel the power of love.
We feel we belong together.
We feel we belong to God.
We feel we belong to God's family.
We are happy.
We are full of joy.
Sing together:
♪   *'The joy of the Lord is my strength.'*
from the Carey Landry album 'Hi God!' (NALR).

PROCLAIM THE GOOD NEWS

In the Holy Book Jesus says:
'If anyone loves me,
he will keep my word,
and my Father will love him,
and we shall come to him,
and make our home with him.'   *John 14:23*

THE MESSAGE

*Go to each person individually, call them by name
and say:*
Tom, Jesus says to you tonight:
'If you love me
I will come to you
and live in you.'
Address the whole group:
Jesus says to all of us here tonight:
'If you love me
I will come to you
and live in you.'

RESPONDING TO THE MESSAGE

*Choose a song to express the joy which friendship
brings.*

Have one of my crisps...

Part I Session 14
WE LISTEN TO THE CALL OF JESUS

AIM
To become aware that Jesus calls us to live with his life.

HUMAN EXPERIENCE
Visiting friends at their house.
Being welcomed into a friend's house.

SPIRITUAL DIMENSION

PREPARATION
For this session you will need:
—the Book of God's Word;
—a candle;
—fresh flowers;

—appropriate music.
You will also need:
—photographs of house/s visited
 with the door open in welcome.

RECALL THE HUMAN EXPERIENCE
I know what John did on Sunday.
John went to tea at Mary's house.
I have a photograph to show you.
There. See. This is where John went.
 Show the photograph to each one.
This is Mary's house.
Look at the door.
 Allow everyone enough time
 to look at the picture and notice the door.
The door is open.
It is open in welcome.
The door is open to let me in.
John, you went in that door...
You went in the door to Mary.
They invited you to come to tea.
Tom, you went to tea with Joan.
 Name the different people who went and how they
 were welcomed.
We have all been welcomed into our friend's home.
We did enjoy being there.
John, you enjoyed being in Mary's home.
 Name each one in relation to their friend.

DEEPEN THE HUMAN EXPERIENCE
Our friends invite us to come to be with them.
We come here to be together.
John comes to be with Mary.
Mary comes to be with John.
Tom comes to be with Joan.
Joan comes to be with Tom.
 Name each one in a similar way.
We want to be with our friends.
Tom wants to be with his friends.

*Mention everyone similarly in relation to their
friend.*
We want to be with the people we love.
We want to be at home with them.

CHURCH DIMENSION

We are together here as friends.
We are happy to be together.
We welcome one another.
We are 'at home' here together.
We love one another.
We are special friends.
Together we gather to listen to Jesus.
Jesus calls us together.
Jesus calls us to be with him.
Jesus calls us.
Jesus calls us to live with his life.
Jesus calls us.
Jesus wants to live in us.
   Pause.
We want to be with Jesus.
We want to be with him.
   Pause.

PROCLAIM THE GOOD NEWS

In the Holy Book Jesus says:
   'Make your home in me.
   I make mine in you.'   *John 15:4 & 7*
   Repeat several times.

THE MESSAGE

   Go to each person, call them by name and say:
Jesus says to you:
   'I make my home in you.
   I live in you.'
   Address the whole group:
Jesus says to all of us here tonight:
   'I make my home in you.
   I live in you.'

Choose an appropriate song or piece of music that will help the group to make the message their own.

Part I—Eucharistic Liturgy

GOD'S PEOPLE TOGETHER

It would be good if the Bishop could be invited, well in advance, to celebrate Mass with the group as they complete Part I of this programme—Building the community.

Part II

WAITING FOR THE SPIRIT

Part II Session 15
SHARING LIFE

AIM

To help each person become aware that Jesus calls us to share
his life.

HUMAN EXPERIENCE

The visit of the Bishop.
The Bishop invited us to share the life of Jesus in the Mass.

SPIRITUAL DIMENSION

PREPARATION

Prepare your special place with:
—the Book of God's Word;
—a candle;
—fresh flowers;
You will also need:
—a photograph of the Bishop, ideally when he came
  to celebrate Mass with group;
—appropriate music.

RECALL THE HUMAN EXPERIENCE

I have brought a photograph of a special friend of ours.
  Show it to the group.
Do you remember who this person is?
Yes, that's our friend Bishop…
  Pass it round.
We had a wonderful evening.
Bishop… came to speak to us before Mass.
Tom, you said 'Hello' to Bishop…
You did too, Joan, and you, Susan…
  Include everyone similarly by name.
We were happy to meet him.
He was pleased to celebrate Mass with us.
He is our friend.
He is Jesus' special friend.
He was happy to be with us.

Recall other aspects of the evening.
It was a great evening.
We all praised God together with the Bishop.
We were happy together.

DEEPEN THE HUMAN EXPERIENCE
We are happy to remember that Mass.
You are happy to remember, Tom.
John is happy.
Address each one individually.
You all look happy.
We are happy to share the memory of that Mass
with our friend Bishop…
We can share what we remember about it together.
We are friends together here.
We share life together here.

CHURCH DIMENSION
When Bishop… came
he invited us to gather near the altar with him.
We prayed with him.
We shared life together.
We share the life of Jesus.
Pause.
When we come here around the Holy Book
we share the life of Jesus.
We listen to Jesus.
Jesus calls us to be his family.
Jesus calls us to share his life.
Pause.

PROCLAIM THE GOOD NEWS
In the Holy Book we read about the time
Jesus called one of his friends to be with him.
Jesus left Capernaum, and as he walked along,
he saw a tax collector, named Matthew, sitting
in his office.

Jesus said to Matthew,
    'Follow me.'   *Matthew 9:9*
Matthew got up and followed Jesus.
Jesus calls us to be his friends.
Jesus calls us to share his life.

THE MESSAGE
*Go to each person individually, call them by name
and say:*
Tom, Jesus says to you tonight:
    'I share my life with you.
    Follow me.'
Address the group as a whole:
Jesus says to all of us tonight:
    'I share my life with you.
    Follow me.'

RESPONDING TO THE MESSAGE
*Choose an appropriate hymn or piece of music which
will help people to assimilate the message.*

The bishop has to be seen as a friend to be significant.

JESUS SHARES HIS SPIRIT WITH US

AIM

To become aware that it is the Spirit of Jesus in us who helps us to love others.

HUMAN EXPERIENCE

The group being together and doing things together over a period of time. The spirit of friendship that exists within the group.

SPIRITUAL DIMENSION

PREPARATION

Prepare your special place with:
—the Book of God's Word;
—a candle;
—fresh flowers;
—appropriate music.
It would be good to have photographs/slides of the group for this session.

RECALL THE HUMAN EXPERIENCE

Show slides or photographs of members of the group being together and doing things together. Allow time for people to really look at and see the slides.

We have been together for a long time now.
Tom, you have been with us for...
And Mary, you have too, and you, Susan.
Name each person, and the length of time they have been in the group.
John, you really belong with us.
Name each one in relation to friend.
I remember when you first came.
Do you remember the first time you came?
I remember when you came, John.
You were shy.

You didn't say very much.
You didn't know us.
*Mention each member of the group and when they
first joined the group.*
We are not shy now.
We have come a long way since we first met.
We feel we know one another now.
I feel I know you, John.
John you feel you know me.
I feel I know Susan.
Susan feels she knows me.
Address each person in a similar way.
We are happy to be together.
We like to be together.
We help one another.
We support one another.
We are good friends now.
We enjoy being together.
I feel we love one another.
You feel that we love one another, don't you, Tom?
You feel that too, Mary.
*Ask each person individually,
and encourage them to respond.*

DEEPEN THE HUMAN EXPERIENCE

When we love one another we feel good together.
I feel I trust Tom.
I trust Susan.
Similarly with each person.
We can get to know one another better.
Tom can get to know Frank.
Mention each person in relation to their friend.
When we love one another we share together.
Then we can love lots of other people.
We can love people in our work centre,
in the hospital, in the hotel...
Name the relevant places.

CHURCH DIMENSION

We are special friends.
John and Frank,
Mary and Frank, *etc.*
We love one another.
We share with one another.
Here together round the Holy Book we are friends.
We prepare to listen to Jesus.
Jesus is our friend.
We are friends of Jesus.
Jesus shares his Spirit of love with us.
Jesus helps us to love one another.
Jesus helps us to love other people.
We listen to what a friend of Jesus says.

PROCLAIM THE GOOD NEWS

In the Holy Book
John, a special friend of Jesus, writes:
'Dear friends,
If this is how God loved us,
then we should love one another.
We are sure that we live in union with God
and that he lives in union with us,
because he has given us his Spirit.'

1 John 4:11 & 13

THE MESSAGE

*Go to each person, take them by the hands,
call them by name and say:*
Tom, Jesus says to you tonight:
'I share my Spirit with you.'
Address the group as a whole:
Jesus says to all of us tonight:
'I share my Spirit with you.'

RESPONDING TO THE MESSAGE

*Choose an appropriate song that will help the group to
express their joy and thanksgiving for the gift of the
Spirit of Jesus.*

Tea with the bishop.

Part II Session 17
JOY

AIM
To help each one become aware of the Spirit in us. The Spirit of Jesus helps us to love one another with joy.

HUMAN EXPERIENCE
Springtime.
*Helping the group to be aware of the **new life** of spring in nature.*

SPIRITUAL DIMENSION

PREPARATION
For this session you will need:
—the Book of God's Word;
—a candle;

RECALL THE HUMAN EXPERIENCE

We went for a lovely walk on Sunday.
What did you like best about it?
There was so much colour.
The daffodils, crocuses, snowdrops, tulips…
John, you saw the daffodils.
Weren't they beautiful?
I have brought some tonight.
They are so lovely.
I feel good.

*Allow time for everyone to say how they feel.
Admire the branches and buds and new life in
a similar way.*

It is a beautiful branch.
It is all new.
It is beautiful.
It is full of life.
It makes me full of joy.
When you see the spring flowers, Tom,
you too are full of joy.
You feel new.
Tom, you feel good in spring.

Address each person individually in a similar way.

The sun comes out now, the days are getting longer.
I feel good.
I want to do my spring cleaning.
I am full of joy.

DEEPEN THE HUMAN EXPERIENCE

I am happy with all of us too.
I am full of joy.
I am so happy to be with Tom,
and Mary and Susan, *etc*.

You give me joy.
We are good friends.
We are happy to be good friends.

CHURCH DIMENSION

Here together we are happy.
We are full of joy.
When we come together here around the Holy Book
our hearts are full of joy.
I want to sing.
Sing a song of joy, for example,
♪ *'Joy, joy, joy',*
from the Carey Landry album 'Hi God!' (NALR).
Let's sing that again.
When I sing:
'I'm so happy, so very happy
I've got the love of Jesus in my heart.'
I am with Jesus.
Pause.
Jesus is with me.
When we sing that we think of Jesus.
We think of the Spirit of Jesus
filling our hearts with joy.
We want to sing again and again:
'I've got that joy, joy, joy, down in my heart etc.'
Sing it again.

PROCLAIM THE GOOD NEWS

In the Holy Book we read that
Jesus, filled with joy by the Holy Spirit, said:
'I bless you, Father, Lord of heaven and earth,
for hiding these things from the learned and the
wise and revealing them to mere children...'

Luke 10:21

THE MESSAGE

Addressing each one say:
Jesus says to you tonight:
'My spirit fills you with joy.'

RESPONDING TO THE MESSAGE

Repeat whatever song of joy you used earlier.

AIM
To help each one realise that Peace is the gift of the Spirit.
**For this session the Human Experience and the Spiritual
Dimension may be combined.*

HUMAN EXPERIENCE
*Saying 'I'm sorry.' Helping each person to tell of a time or
an occasion when they said 'I'm sorry.' Allow people time
to remember and to tell their story. Help those who find it
difficult to express themselves.*

SPIRITUAL DIMENSION

PREPARATION
For this session you will need:
—the Book of God's Word;
—a candle;
—fresh flowers;
—appropriate music.

RECALL THE HUMAN EXPERIENCE
As above.

DEEPEN THE HUMAN EXPERIENCE
When I say 'I'm sorry' my friend forgives me.
My friend smiles.
He/she says 'It's all right.'
I'm happy again.
I have peace.
My heart is full of peace.
I am happy again.
I am full of joy.
When Tom says 'I'm sorry' his friend forgives him.
He/she says 'That's OK, Tom.'
Tom, you are happy.
Your heart is full of joy.

You have peace.
Mary, when you say 'I'm sorry' you feel happy inside.
When you are forgiven you have peace.
Your heart is full of joy.
Address each person, stressing 'I'm sorry,'
being forgiven and being at peace.

CHURCH DIMENSION

When we come together with the priest at Mass
he helps us to say 'I'm sorry.'
With the priest we say 'I confess.'
Say the Confiteor slowly.
With the priest we are together as one family.
The priest says:
'May Almighty God have mercy on you,
forgive you your sins.'
We are happy again.
We are one again.
Our hearts are full of joy.
We have peace.
Pause.
Get up slowly and move to pick up the Holy Book.
Do so deliberately and reverently.

PROCLAIM THE GOOD NEWS

Introduce and read John 20:19-23.

THE MESSAGE

John, Jesus says to you tonight:
'Peace be with you.
My peace I give you.'

RESPONDING TO THE MESSAGE

Choose a suitable 'Peace' song that the group can
listen to and/or sing together. For example,
♪   'Peacetime'
from the Carey Landry album 'Hi God!' (NALR);
Folk Hymnal Volume 4, no. 37.

Part II Session 19
THE SPIRIT BRINGS LOVE

AIM
To help each member of the faith community become aware of
our longing for the Holy Spirit. It is the Spirit of Jesus who fills
us with his love.

HUMAN EXPERIENCE
Care of self: *Devote time to help the handicapped person
to acquire or develop a particular skill: e.g. grooming,
make-up, dressing up for a special occasion and using
perfume or cologne.*
More than one session could well be given to this.

SPIRITUAL DIMENSION

PREPARATION
For this session you will need:
—the Book of God's Word;
—a candle;
—fresh flowers;
—appropriate music.
*You will also need perfume and/or cologne for both
the girls and the boys.*

RECALL THE HUMAN EXPERIENCE
*Help each person to share how he/she felt when
he/she dressed up for a special event.*
Allow people plenty of time.
Mary uses perfume. I know.
I can smell the lovely fragrance.
What is it called?
And you Tom, you use Brut.
Or whatever.
Address each person in the group in a similar way.
I'd like to share my perfume with you all.
I am going to put some on Mary's hands.
Now we can all smell the perfume.

Can you smell it, Tom?
and you, Joan?
    Ask each one in the group.
It smells nice. Really nice.
Let me put some on you too, Joan.
    Give some to everybody.
Now the perfume smells stronger.
It fills our circle.
It fills the room.
It smells so good.
I like to stay near you.
You all smell so nice.

DEEPEN THE HUMAN EXPERIENCE

The smell of perfume attracts us.
Such a nice fragrance attracts us.
Such a fragrance fills the room, fills us.
It smells so nice.
It fills us.
It makes everyone feel so beautiful.
It makes us beautiful.

CHURCH DIMENSION

When we come here we gather round the Holy Book.
Each one of us chooses to come here.
You come, Tom, because you want to be here
with your friends.
    Address each person.
We choose to come.
Each one of us here says: 'Yes, I want to be here.'
The Spirit of Jesus attracts us.
The Spirit of Jesus calls us to come
together here around the Holy Book.
    Pause.
When we gather here around the Holy Book
the Spirit of Jesus draws us together.
The Spirit of Jesus is with us.
The Spirit of Jesus fills us.
We want to stay together here.

The Spirit of Jesus fills our hearts with love.
He brings us love.
Pause.
This pause could be enhanced by suitable
classical music.

PROCLAIM THE GOOD NEWS
Introduce the scripture reading:
In the Holy Book, a friend of Jesus says:
then read Ephesians 3:14-19.

THE MESSAGE
Go to each person individually,
address them by name and say:
Jesus says to you tonight:
'I live in you.'

RESPONDING TO THE MESSAGE
Choose an appropriate piece of music to bring the
session to a close.

Part II Session 20
TOGETHER IN THE SPIRIT

AIM
To help each person become aware of the Spirit of Jesus
within them.
When we come together as believing people the Holy Spirit of
love is poured into our hearts. It is the Spirit who turns us
towards God our Father.

HUMAN EXPERIENCE
Friends enjoying the beauty of nature together whether
through a visit to a park or admiring flowers and plants
in the room where the group usually meets.

SPIRITUAL DIMENSION

PREPARATION

For this session you will need:
—the Book of God's Word;
—a candle;
—fresh flowers;
—appropriate music.
In addition to the fresh flowers, you will need a
houseplant.

RECALL THE HUMAN EXPERIENCE

What lovely flowers!

Help the group as a whole and each person
individually to focus on the flowers:
colour, smell, variety, feel.
Draw attention to the damp stems.

The scent fills the room.
Isn't it beautiful?
These flowers are beautiful.
They are so fresh.

Pause.

And this plant.
This is beautiful too.
Look how big it is getting.
It was only a tiny plant when we started coming
together here, wasn't it?
Do you remember, Tom?

Draw each person individually into your
conversation about the plants.

It's big now because we take care of it.
We keep it watered.
Let's pour in some water now.

Water the plant slowly.
Make sure everyone can see what you are doing.

See how the water disappears into the earth.
We cannot see it anymore.
But the water <u>inside</u> makes the plant grow.
Our plant is growing.

We are happy to see it grow.
We like to come together near the plant.
We are friends together here.
Because we are friends, we help one another.
Bill helps Jim.
*Mention each helper and friend in relation to
one another.*
Now we are all friends.
Pause.

DEEPEN THE HUMAN EXPERIENCE

Friends help each other.
Friends help each other to grow.
We help each other to grow by being happy <u>inside</u>.
We encourage one another.
We help one another to grow.

CHURCH DIMENSION

When we come together in our special place
we help one another to grow.
When we are together here,
Jesus is with us.
Jesus gives us his Holy Spirit.
We do not see him, but deep inside us,
he helps us to grow.
Deep inside us he helps us to be happy.
He helps us to love one another.
The Holy Spirit of Jesus is in us, deep within us.
The Holy Spirit is in you, Tom.
Name each person, helper and friend.
At Pentecost we celebrate the Holy Spirit,
the Holy Spirit who comes to fill us with life.

PROCLAIM THE GOOD NEWS

In the Holy Book, Jesus tells us about his Spirit.
Jesus says:
'I will ask the Father,
and he will give you another Helper,
who will stay with you for ever.

He is the Spirit.
You know him,
because he remains with you
and is in you.'   *John 14:16 & 17*

THE MESSAGE

Go to each person, call them by name and say:
Tom, Jesus says to you tonight:
'My Spirit is in you.'
Address the group as a whole:
Jesus says to all of us tonight:
'My Spirit is in you.'

RESPONDING TO THE MESSAGE

Listen together to the song, and sing
♪   *'Spirit of the living God'*
Folk Hymnal Volume 2, no. 69;
Songs of the Spirit, no. 76;
Hymns Old & New, no. 250;
Hymns Old & New Enlarged, no. 501.

Part II—Eucharistic Liturgy

CELEBRATING OUR LIFE IN THE SPIRIT

On the basis of the sessions they have shared so far, the group
should prepare and celebrate together a eucharistic liturgy on
the theme of 'celebrating our life in the Spirit.'

Part II Session 21
SHARING THE SPIRIT OF LIFE

AIM

To help each person realise that it is through the human experience of friendship that we share the life of God's Spirit.

HUMAN EXPERIENCE

The friendship developed between each helper and friend and within the group as a whole.

SPIRITUAL DIMENSION

PREPARATION

For this session you will need:
—the Book of God's Word;
—fresh flowers;
—a candle;
—appropriate music.

RECALL THE HUMAN EXPERIENCE

John, Tom, Mary, Susan…
　　Name everybody.
I am so glad that you are here tonight.
I was waiting for you.
I knew you would come.
Do you remember when we first met?
Do you remember Tom and Bill?
I was hoping that you would come then.
Do you remember Mary and Susan?
　　Address each friend and helper in a similar way.
Tonight I knew you would come.
We have been friends now for a long time.
We are good friends.
Tom and Bill are friends.
Mary and Susan are friends.
　　Name helpers and friends in relation to one another.
We are all friends together.
That's good, isn't it?

It's good to be friends.
It's good to have a friend.
Allow the group to comment.
We've done lots of things since we came together.
What have you enjoyed most?
Give everyone time to respond.
I love being with all my friends.
I am happy to be with my friends.
I am happy to be with Tom and Bill.
Name each helper and friend.
Pause.

DEEPEN THE HUMAN EXPERIENCE

When we are together as friends
we feel good, we feel great.
We feel alive.
When we are together as friends
we can chat, sing, have a party, an outing.
We can also be quiet together.
We can pray together.
When we are together as friends
we are able to share.
We are able to be one.
When we share together
we are able to be one in the Spirit.
We want to stay together.

CHURCH DIMENSION

When we had Mass with Father...
Name the priest, the place and the day.
we were together round the altar.
We came together with the priest.
We prayed and sang together.
We were quiet together.
When we gather together at Mass
we share the Holy Bread or Communion.
Jesus fills us with his life.
Jesus stays with us in his Spirit.
We are one in his Spirit.

PROCLAIM THE GOOD NEWS

In the Holy Book, a friend of Jesus writes:
    'Since the Spirit is our life,
    let us be led by the Spirit.'   *Galatians 5:25*
Repeat several times.

THE MESSAGE

Go to each person, call them by name and say:
Tom, Jesus says to you tonight:
    'My Spirit is in you.
    My Spirit gives you life.'
Address the group as a whole:
Jesus says to all of us tonight:
    'My Spirit is in you.
    My Spirit gives you life.'

RESPONDING TO THE MESSAGE

Sing together
♪   *'We are one in the Spirit.'*
Folk Hymnal Volume 1, no. 46;
Hymns Old & New, no. 294.

Helping the bishop to clean his crozier for the confirmation ceremony.

THE SPIRIT MOVES US TOWARDS THE FULLNESS OF LIFE

AIM
To become aware of the Spirit urging us towards union with
God the Father in Jesus.

HUMAN EXPERIENCE
*The weather as we experience it in this country: too cold,
too wet, and not enough sunshine!*

SPIRITUAL DIMENSION

PREPARATION
For this session you will need:
—the Book of God's Word;
—a candle;
—fresh flowers;
—appropriate music.

RECALL THE HUMAN EXPERIENCE
I feel cold today.
You look cold too.
> *Involve people, mentioning them by name.*

Our weather is sometimes hard to put up with.
We don't get too much sunshine, do we?
It can be cold.
It can be very wet.
When it's windy I find it a struggle to walk.
John, you find it difficult to walk when it's windy,
don't you?
> *Draw everyone into the discussion.*
> *Encourage them to share their experiences of*
> *weather.*

But we survive, don't we?
We put up with the weather when we can't enjoy it.
We keep going.
We go out to work, to the training centre,
to the shops, in spite of the weather.

Life goes on in spite of the weather, doesn't it?
Pause
When our work is hard,
even when we get bored,
we keep going.
We know that we are moving towards better days.
We know that when Spring (*or* Summer) comes,
the weather will be better.
We are moving towards a time of new life,
a time when we will have more energy for living
more energy for giving.
We know in our hearts
that we move towards a time of new life,
a time of fullness in life.
Pause.

DEEPEN THE HUMAN EXPERIENCE

Knowing that better days are coming
helps us to keep going.
It helps us to get through the day, the week,
it helps us through life.
We move towards new life.
The Spirit within us moves us towards life.

CHURCH DIMENSION

When we go to Mass
we pray together with the priest:
'Lord, have mercy.
Christ, have mercy.
Lord, have mercy.'
The Spirit within us urges us towards life.
We offer ourselves to the Lord.
Jesus accepts our offering.
With Jesus we ask for life.

PROCLAIM THE GOOD NEWS

In the Holy Book the Spirit of God urges all the
people of God towards life.

> *Go to each person, call them by name and say:*
> Tom, Jesus says to you tonight:
> 'I promise you the fullness of life.'
> *Address the whole group:*
> Jesus says to all of us gathered together here:
> 'I promise you the fullness of life.'

RESPONDING TO THE MESSAGE

> *Choose a suitable piece of music that focuses on the theme of 'new life,' and will give the group an opportunity to sing praise and thanksgiving for the new life in the Spirit that they share.*
> *for example:*
> ♪   *'New life!'*
> *from the Carey Landry album 'I will not forget you' (NALR);*
> *Folk Hymnal Volume 4, no. 18;*
> *Hymns Old & New Enlarged, no. 371.*

Part II Session 23
THE SPIRIT BRINGS JOY

AIM

To become aware of the joy that comes from the Spirit of God. When we share together we know the joy of the Kingdom that is both here and now and yet is still to come.

HUMAN EXPERIENCE

> *For this session choose events that lead to or encourage these experiences:*
> *—being happy **together**.*
> *—**sharing** something that everyone can enjoy;*
> *—**knowing** that the event will mean a lot to everybody.*

SPIRITUAL DIMENSION

PREPARATION

Prepare your special place with:
—the Book of God's Word;
—a candle;
—fresh flowers;
—appropriate music.

RECALL THE HUMAN EXPERIENCE

*Recall the time when the members of the group were
engaged in an event that led to a shared experience.
Recall the event or occasion as vividly as possible
(use photographs, slides, if you can) so that each
person will relive the experience fully.*

DEEPEN THE HUMAN EXPERIENCE

I shall remember for a long time
the wonderful time we had together.
I feel very happy that I could be with you all.
When I am with you I am happy.
When I see your goodness and when you share
with me I feel strong.
When we share something beautiful together
we grow strong.
We know that we are not alone.
We are filled with joy.
We know that the goodness which is all around us
is our strength.
   Pause.

CHURCH DIMENSION

When we come together at Mass with Father...
we take part in the prayer of Jesus.
We share our joy in the Lord.
The Spirit of the Lord fills our hearts with joy.
We share the Bread of the Lord.
We share the joy of the Lord.
We know that the Holy Spirit gives us this joy.
We know that our joy is the Lord.
We know that the Lord is our strength.

PROCLAIM THE GOOD NEWS
> In the Holy Book we read:
> > 'I rejoice because of what the Lord has done.
> > God has clothed me with salvation and victory.'
>
> *Isaiah 61:10*

THE MESSAGE
> *Go to each person individually,*
> *address them by name and say:*
> Jesus says to you tonight:
> > 'I am your joy.
> > I am your strength.'

RESPONDING TO THE MESSAGE
> *Listen to and/or sing together:*
> ♪   *'The joy of the Lord.'*
> *from the Carey Landry album 'Hi God!' (NALR).*

Part II Session 24
THE SPIRIT PRAYS IN US

AIM
To be aware that we respond to the message of the Lord
through the Spirit who prays in us.

HUMAN EXPERIENCE
Blowing bubbles!
This is something that we can enjoy together as a group
of adults with our friends. Depending on how we present
it, blowing bubbles can either be a childish thing or
a moment of wonder and awe. Let's make it the latter.
Take time to enter into the wonder of what is happening.
Have this experience on a day when there is a little wind.
Be open enough to enjoy the colour of the bubbles and
their movement as they gently soar upwards and away.

SPIRITUAL DIMENSION

PREPARATION
For this session you need:
—the Book of God's Word;
—flowers;
—a candle;
—slides or photographs of the group blowing bubbles;
—appropriate music.

RECALL THE HUMAN EXPERIENCE
I have some photographs/slides to show you.
I took them when we were enjoying ourselves on...
Name the day, place
—any detail that will help everyone to remember.
What a wonderful time we had blowing bubbles.
Look at John.
Show the slide or photograph.
Allow everyone time to see it
and to notice what is happening.
Isn't that wonderful?
What a huge bubble you had, John.
Can you see the colour?
Look closely.
Yes, it's there.
It's very delicate, isn't it?
Proceed in the same way,
showing all the slides/photographs
and commenting on each one.
For example:
See how the bubbles are up in the air.
It was a windy day, wasn't it?
The wind helped to blow our bubbles up into the air.
Some of our bubbles went up, up, up and away.
Gesture the upward movement.
They went up so high.
Gesture.
We couldn't catch them.
The wind carried them up into the sky.

Didn't they look beautiful and wonderful?
Address each person and allow time for a response.

DEEPEN THE HUMAN EXPERIENCE
I was so happy blowing bubbles.
I was glad there was some wind.
John, you were glad, weren't you?
Draw everyone into the discussion.
with similar questions and comments.
We are all happy that there was a gentle wind.
The wind lifted the bubbles up into the air.
Gesture this upwards movement several times.
The wind carried our bubbles up, up, up and away
into the air.
We were happy.
You were happy, John. Yes.
Mention everyone individually and allow them time
to say or show how they felt.
We were really happy together.
Pause.

CHURCH DIMENSION
When we come together here we are happy.
You are happy, John.
Address each person in the group.
Help them to express how they feel now at this
moment,
if necessary by saying it for them.
We are happy together.
There is a place for each of us here.
There is a place for John.
There is a place for Mary.
Name each one in a similar way.
Here around the Holy Book
Point towards it.
there is a place for each one of us.
We are happy here.
We are friends here.
We prepare our hearts to listen to Jesus.

Jesus is with us.
We are happy.
We are with Jesus.
We are happy.
Jesus is with us.
We sing a song of joy.
Sing a joyful hymn familiar to the group.
Pause.
We wait.
We wait together to listen to Jesus.
Jesus is with us here around the Holy Book.
Jesus speaks to us in the Holy Book.
We wait.
I am waiting.
John is waiting.
Name each person.
We are all waiting together to listen to Jesus.
We lift up our hearts.
Gesture.
We stand up.
We reach up in praise.
Use appropriate gestures.
Jesus is with us.
We sing.
Repeat song.
The spirit of Jesus carries our joy
and lifts our song of praise to God our Father.
Pause.

PROCLAIM THE GOOD NEWS
In the Holy Book we read:
'The Spirit comes
to help us in our weakness.
When we cannot find words we need to pray properly
the Spirit himself helps us
in a way that could never be put into words.'

Go to each person, call them by name and say:
John, Jesus says to you today:
'My Spirit in you
lifts up your prayer to the Father.'
Help each person to make an appropriate gesture.
Address the group as a whole:
Jesus says to all of us here today:
'My Spirit in you
lifts up your prayer to the Father.'
Again, use gesture.

RESPONDING TO THE MESSAGE

*Repeat the previous song of joy or choose another
which expresses praise and thanksgiving. Use
gestures as you sing to help each person to enter into
the movement of praise and to bring the explicitly
spiritual part of the session to a close. For example,*
♪ *'Alleluia to our God'*
*from the Carey Landry album 'Bloom where you are
planted.' (NALR).*

Part II Session 25
THE SPIRIT GIVES US COURAGE

AIM
To become aware that the Spirit of God gives us strength to
be faithful to the call of Jesus.

HUMAN EXPERIENCE

*The experience of being misunderstood, left out and even
rejected. This is a very real experience for many of our
friends.*

SPIRITUAL DIMENSION

PREPARATION

Prepare your special corner with:
—the Book of God's Word;

—a candle;
—fresh flowers.
You will also need appropriate music.

RECALL THE HUMAN EXPERIENCE
It's good to be with all my friends again.
Sometimes being friends with other people isn't easy.
It's true, isn't it?
Some people don't want to be friends.
They don't want to be friends with us.
>   *Pause.*
You know this, Tom, don't you?
>   *Allow time for sharing on this point.*
>   *Help those who find it difficult.*
We know this from work.
Some people at work don't accept us.
When we go to the training centre
this happens sometimes.
Or when we go shopping,
or when we go for a walk along the street,
we feel people don't want to know us.
Even when we go to church
this sometimes happens.
>   *Pause.*
We smile at them—
but they don't smile at us.
John, you like to smile at people.
>   *Mention everyone individually,*
>   *draw them into the discussion.*
We try to be kind, to understand.
Sometimes people try to understand us, too.
But they don't.
They can't accept us as friends.
They're not able.
>   *Try to get concrete examples from the group—*
>   *helpers and friends.*

It makes us sad, doesn't it?
When we try to be friends with others,
but they won't let us,
we feel sad and lonely.
You sometimes feel sad, Mary.
> *Draw a response from everyone in the group.*

Maybe we should stay at home,
and not go out at all.
Would you like that, Tom?
> *Ask everyone a similar question.*

Should we stop trying to be friends with others?
Should we stay away from work?
Should we stop going to church?
Is this the right thing to do?
Do you think it right, Tom?
> *Elicit responses from individuals*
> *and from the group.*
> *Pause.*

We need courage.
We need courage to keep trying.
We need courage.
Some people might not accept us as their friends.
We need courage to continue to work, to pray,
to go out to others.
We need courage to give ourselves every day to
our work.
We need strength in our hearts
so that we can continue to do
what we are called to do every day.

CHURCH DIMENSION

When we gather around the altar with the priest,
we ask for the courage to love.
We receive Holy Communion.
Jesus is with us.
The Spirit of Jesus is with us.
We trust in the Spirit of Jesus.

One day Jesus talked to his friends.
He said:
>'If anyone wants to come with me,
>he must forget self,
>take up his cross every day,
>and follow me.' *Luke 9:23*
>'The Spirit that God has given us
>does not make us timid;
>instead, his Spirit fills us
>with power, love and self-control.' *2 Timothy 1:7*

Jesus calls us to love.
Jesus gives us his Spirit.
The Spirit of Jesus gives us the courage to love.

THE MESSAGE

>*Go to each person individually, call them by name and say:*
>Tom, Jesus says to you tonight:
>>'I give you my Spirit.'
>>*Address the group as a whole:*
>Jesus says to us all tonight:
>>'I give you my Spirit.'

RESPONDING TO THE MESSAGE

>*Sing together*
>♪   *'Spirit of the living God.'*
>*Folk Hymnal Volume 2, no. 69;*
>*Songs of the Spirit, no. 76;*
>*Hymns Old & New, no. 250;*
>*Hymns Old & New Enlarged, no. 501.*

Part II Session 26
SPIRIT OF LIFE

AIM

To become aware that we need a force greater than ourselves
to penetrate our weaknesses, our suffering. Through confirmation we are equipped for full sharing in the eucharistic celebration of a people filled with the Spirit of Jesus.

HUMAN EXPERIENCE

Sport:
—ideally by personal participation in sport of some kind;
—alternatively, spectating at sport, even if only on the television.

SPIRITUAL DIMENSION

PREPARATION

Prepare your special place with:
—the Book of God's Word;
—a candle;
—fresh flowers;
—appropriate music.

RECALL THE HUMAN EXPERIENCE

Depending on what the actual experience was, help each person to talk about the experience and help each one to name his favourite sport.

We always want our team to win, don't we?
We cheer and try to help them on to win.
But sometimes our team doesn't do too well.
Sometimes our team loses.
They have a bad day.
They can't do what they need to do to win.
They are disappointed.
Pause.
Sometimes we have a bad day too.
Have you had a bad day lately, Bill?
Let a helper talk about such an experience and draw in the handicapped person.
Things don't always go right do they?
Sometimes we feel bad.
We feel disappointed, upset.
Pause.

DEEPEN THE HUMAN EXPERIENCE

When we don't succeed we feel disappointed.
We look for encouragement.
We need a friend.
We need to share our disappointment with a friend.
Pause.

CHURCH DIMENSION

Here we are friends.
When we come together here we are all friends.
Tom and Bill are friends.
Mention each person in relation to their friend.
We belong together.
We help one another.
We acknowledge one another.
We listen to one another.
We come together to listen to God's Word.
The Spirit of Jesus gives us courage.
The Spirit of Jesus gives us strength
to overcome our disappointments.
The Spirit of Jesus helps us
to live as children of God.

PROCLAIM THE GOOD NEWS

In the Holy Book a friend of Jesus says:
'The love of God has been poured into our hearts
by the Holy Spirit which has been given to us.'

Romans 5:5

'We are children of God.
We share his sufferings so that
we can also share his glory.'   *Romans 8:17*

THE MESSAGE

Go to each person, call them by name and say:
Tom, Jesus says to you tonight:
'My Spirit will give you courage.'
Address the group as a whole:
Jesus says to all of us tonight:
'My Spirit will give you courage.'

103

Choose hymns of praise and thanksgiving to help the group to penetrate the mystery.

Part II Session 27
CONFIRMED IN THE SPIRIT

AIM

To become aware of the anointing of the Holy Spirit which confirms us within and with one another so that we may be full of life, love and gratitude.

HUMAN EXPERIENCE

Being hurt and recovering after a physical injury, seeing cuts and bruises heal.

SPIRITUAL DIMENSION

PREPARATION

Prepare your special place with:
—the Book of God's Word;
—a candle;
—fresh flowers;
—appropriate music.
For this session you will also need:
—holy oil (make sure it is fresh!);
—cotton wool;
—a photograph of the bishop who will confirm the handicapped person/s.

RECALL THE HUMAN EXPERIENCE

Recall the healing process
by getting members of the group to speak about being hurt and getting better.
My finger is almost better.
It had a deep cut.
The doctor gave me some oil to put on it.
It is almost healed.
Pause.

Pause.

I have something special to show you.
It is in this lovely jar.
Let's open it carefully.
It's precious. There!
It smells good.

Smell it.

Would you like to smell it, Tom?

Give everyone the opportunity to smell the oil.

I am going to put some on this cotton wool.
Now I am going to put it on my cut finger.
Look.
It feels good.
That will heal my wound.
Has anyone else got a cut?
Would you like some oil?
Here you are.

Pause.

When my hands hurt me I put cream and oil on them.
When I burn myself I put oil on the part that hurts.
Then the sore part starts to heal.
It doesn't hurt any more.
It feels good.
I can move my hand easily.
I can move my hand easily again.
I am really grateful.

Pause.

Sometimes my feelings get hurt too.

Give a concrete example.

I feel miserable.
Then someone is kind to me.
My friend is kind to me.
I feel a lot better.
I feel grateful.

*Encourage the group to talk about having their
feelings hurt by others. Allow enough time for all
to contribute to the discussion.*

DEEPEN THE HUMAN EXPERIENCE

We are all friends.
We are kind to one another.
Mention each person in the group
and any acts of kindness
witnessed in the group over a period of time.
We are happy to be together.
We are glad to be together.
We feel at peace with one another.
We have peace.
We are grateful.

CHURCH DIMENSION

Soon a special friend of ours will come to our parish.
Our special friend is Bishop…
Show his photograph to the group.
He is a special friend of Jesus, too.
When Bishop… comes to us
he will put oil on your forehead.
He will put beautiful oil on your forehead like this.
Go to each person to be confirmed
and make the Sign of the Cross
on each one's forehead.
When the Bishop puts the holy oil on you, John,
we will pray that the Holy Spirit of love
will make you strong and full of life.
Mention each person to be confirmed in the
same way.

PROCLAIM THE GOOD NEWS

Use the reading from the Confirmation Mass.
(See page 114.)

THE MESSAGE

Go to each person, lay your hands on their head,
call them by name, and say:
John, Jesus says to you:
'I give you my Spirit.'
Address the group as a whole:

Jesus says to all of us:
'I give you my Spirit.'

RESPONDING TO THE MESSAGE

Use the song:
♪ *'Spirit of the living God.'*
Folk Hymnal Volume 2, no. 69;
Songs of the Spirit, no. 76;
Hymns Old & New, no. 250;
Hymns Old & New Enlarged, no. 501.
Expand the song by using not only the words, but
instruments and gestures as well.

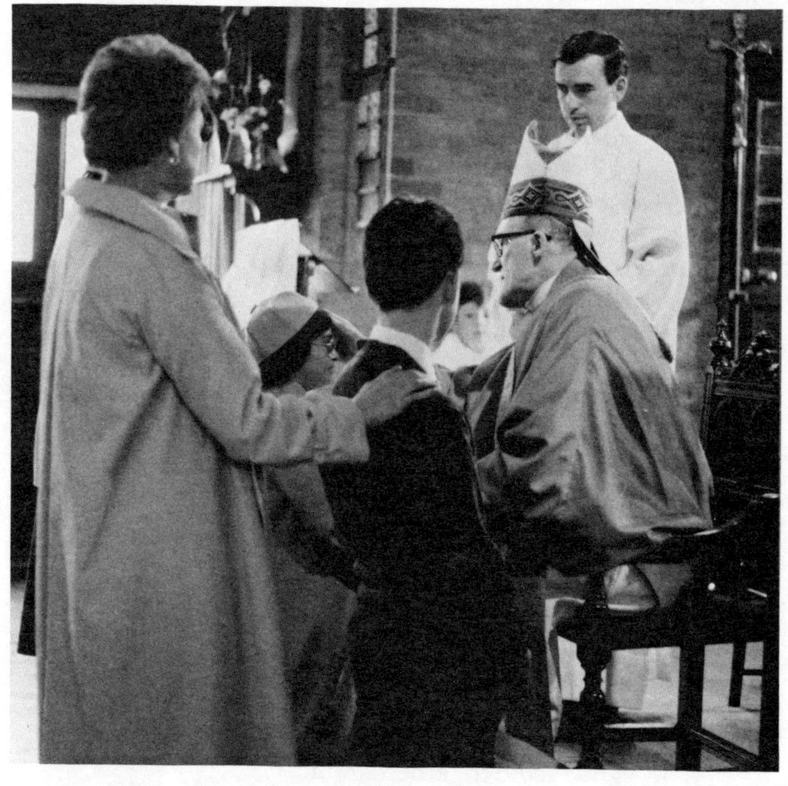

Confirmed in the Spirit.

AIM

To become aware of our intimacy with the Spirit of Jesus and to celebrate the 'wholeness' we are called to through the sacrament of reconciliation. Praying for healing and celebrating wholeness is not the prerogative of the priest. It is the duty of all the ordinary people of God—you and me. It is fitting that a group of believing people who have grown together humanly and spiritually over a period of time should gather with the priest to celebrate 'wholeness'. The members of this little faith community are natural channels of healing for one another. In fact the greeting in the new rite invites all people to use the healing power of Jesus in praying for the needs of one another.

PREPARATION

Prepare the place for celebration. You will need:
—the Book of God's Word;
—a candle;
—fresh flowers.
The celebrant will need to bring:
—holy oil;
—an alb and a stole.

OPENING HYMN

A hymn of praise familiar to your group, for example,
♪   *'Sing praises to the living God'*
Folk Hymnal Volume 2, no. 10;
Hymns Old & New Enlarged, no. 490.

PENITENTIAL RITE

The celebrant begins the penitential rite
by inviting the group to stand in a circle
and to hold hands.
The celebrant says:
It's good to be together again.
It's good to be with our friends.

When we are like this we are all joined, one to another.
When we hold hands we are joined, one to another.
Joined together, we move together.
Move slowly, getting all to do likewise.
You could include a simple dance here if this is
possible.
All joined together we are friends.
Pause.
Sometimes we are not friends.
Hands by your side;
lead the group to do likewise.
I am all on my own.
John, you are all on your own.
Mary, you are all on your own.
Mention each person.
I am alone.
Encourage each person individually
to acknowledge 'I am alone'.
We are alone.
Sometimes I'm sad.
Gesture of hands over face.
The catechist will help the handicapped person
to do the same.
John is sad.
Mention each one by name individually.
We are sad.
Pause.
I have no friend to be with me.
Walk round aimlessly.
Turn to a catechist, and address him/her in a
similar way:
Joan, you have no friend to be with.
The catechist walks round aimlessly.
Address each person in the group in a similar way.
I turn my back on my friends.
Turn your back to group.
I turn my back on Tony.
John turns his back on his friends.

*The catechist will help the handicapped person
to do this.*
Mary turns her back on her friends.
Mention each one.
We turn our backs on our friends.
Gesture.
We feel unhappy.
Pause.
We need our friends.
We need to say sorry.
We need to be forgiven.
*The celebrant approaches each person in turn,
calls them by name and says:*
Are you sorry for turning your back on your friends?
*Allow each person enough time to respond properly
either in words or gesture.
The celebrant then addresses the group as a whole:*
Will you try to love others?
All respond, with help if necessary:
We will.

ABSOLUTION

*The celebrant goes to each person,
places his hand on their head
and prays the words of absoloution.
After receiving forgiveness the members of the group
exchange a Sign of Peace with one another.
Meanwhile, sing together:*
♪   *'Lay your hands gently upon us'
Folk Hymnal Volume 4, no. 44;
Songs of the Spirit, no. 87;
Hymns Old & New, no. 144;
Hymns Old & New Enlarged, no. 295.*

LITURGY OF THE WORD

In the Holy Book, Jesus says to us:
'I give you a new commandment:
love one another;

just as I have loved you,
you also must love one another.'   *John 13:34*
    Pause, then repeat:
'Love one another;
just as I have loved you,
you must also love one another.'

THE MESSAGE

*In the same way as in the sessions, the celebrant
goes to each person individually, addresses them
by name and says:*
John, Jesus says to you today:
'I love you.
Love one another.'
The celebrant then addresses the whole group:
Jesus says to all of us here tonight:
'I love you.
Love one another.'
Allow a reflective pause.
*Classical music might help people to assimilate
the message:*
Fade out music gradually.

BLESSING WITH HOLY OIL

*The celebrant shows the holy oil to the group.
Allow time for each one to see it, to smell it, to
touch it.
The celebrant then says:*
When Bishop… comes to confirm you
he will put oil on your forehead like this.
    *Go to each one,
    make the Sign of the Cross on their forehead
    and hands and say:*
Through this holy oil
may the Spirit of Jesus
give you courage
to speak the words of Jesus to others.
Go, bring 'Good News' to everyone you meet.

Sing together:
♪ *'Our God reigns'*
Songs of the Spirit, no. 29;
More Songs of the Spirit, no. 134;
Hymns Old & New Enlarged, no. 223 or 224

PRAYER OF PRAISE AND THANKSGIVING

On behalf of all, the celebrant prays:
God our Father,
we praise and thank you for bringing us together
today.
We thank you for one another.
We thank you for all those who offer us their
friendship.
We praise and thank you above all
for sending Jesus to live among us
and to bring us your forgiveness.
We praise and thank you for the Holy Spirit
who is in us and who will come to us in a special way
in confirmation.
We offer you our praise and our thanks
through Jesus your Son,
Who lives and reigns with you and the Holy Spirit,
one God, for ever and ever.
All respond:
Amen.

FINAL HYMN
♪ *'God's Spirit is in my heart'*
Folk Hymnal Volume 1, no. 57;
Hymns Old & New, no. 89;
Hymns Old & New Enlarged, no. 183.
Invite the celebrant to share some light
refreshments with you after this celebration.

Part II—The Celebration of Confirmation
THE COMING OF THE SPIRIT

The Introduction to the Rite of Confirmation says that normally 'Confirmation takes place within Mass to express more clearly the fundamental connection of this sacrament with the entirety of Christian initiation. The latter reaches its culmination in the communion of the body and blood of Christ. The newly confirmed should therefore participate in the Eucharist which completes their Christian initiation.' (Praenotanda, 13)

The following liturgy is not so much a special liturgy for mentally handicapped people but rather an integrated one at which all those to be confirmed, and their families, can fully participate. Our aim has been to produce a liturgy to include members of the parish community who suffer from one form of disability or another.

INTRODUCTORY RITES

PROCESSIONAL HYMN
Sing an appropriate hymn in which all can join in.

GREETING
In the name of the Father...
(*as usual*).
Welcome to you all.
Welcome to you, parents
who have come with sons and daughters.
Welcome to you young people, children, friends.
Welcome to those of you who live in hospitals or homes
or hostels.
I'm happy to be with you today
as we prepare together for the coming of the Holy Spirit.

PENITENTIAL RITE
Celebrate it in whatever way suits the group best.

GLORIA

Let us now praise God together in this joyful song:
♪ *'Peruvian Gloria'*
Folk Hymnal Volume 2, no. 75;
Hymns Old & New, no. 81;
Hymns Old & New Enlarged, no. 167.

OPENING PRAYER

From the rite of confirmation.

LITURGY OF THE WORD

GOSPEL GREETING

As the Book of the Gospels is taken in solemn procession to the
Bishop, all sing:
♪ *'Spirit of the living God'*
Folk Hymnal Volume 2, no. 69;
Hymns Old & New, no. 250;
Hymns Old & New Enlarged, no. 501.

PROCLAMATION OF THE GOSPEL

The Lord be with you.
All respond: And also with you.
A Reading from the Gospel according to John.
All respond: Glory to you, Lord.
In the evening Jesus came to his friends.
He said to them:
'Peace be with you.'
His friends were filled with joy.
Jesus said to them again:
'Peace be with you.'
Then he said:
'Receive the Holy Spirit.'
His friends were filled with joy.
'Receive the Holy Spirit,' Jesus said.
His friends were filled with joy.
Hold the Book up for all to see.
This is the Gospel of the Lord
All respond: Praise to you, Lord Jesus Christ.

PRESENTATION OF THE CANDIDATES

The parish priest presents the candidates:
At this time we would like to present our friends
who will be gifted in a special way today.
He calls the names of all to be confirmed.
Each one stands as his name is called.
At the end all clap.

HOMILY

The Bishop gives the message of the Gospel to all.
Jesus says to you today: *He turns to right.*
   'I give you my Spirit.
   I give you my joy.'
Jesus says to you today: *He turns to left.*
   'I give you my Spirit.
   I give you my joy.'
Jesus says to you today: *He turns to centre aisle.*
   'I give you my Spirit.
   I give you my joy.'
Finally
Jesus says to all of us here today:
   'I give you my Spirit.
   I give you my joy.'

PROFESSION OF FAITH

Together let us proclaim our faith.
Do you believe that Jesus wants you to be happy?
Response: We believe.
Do you believe that with Jesus you can learn to love others?
Response: We believe.
Do you believe that with Jesus we can change our hearts?
Response: We believe.
Do you believe that Jesus came to tell us about God whom
he loves?
Response: We believe.
Do you believe that Jesus gives us his Holy Spirit to help us
to live as children of God?
Response: We believe.

THE SACRAMENT OF CONFIRMATION

*The sacrament is celebrated as in the rite of confirmation.
If there are many candidates, suitable songs should be sung
during the actual confirmations.*

LITURGY OF THE EUCHARIST

PRESENTATION & PREPARATION OF THE GIFTS
*Involve some of those to be confirmed and their families/
friends in the offertory procession.
A suitable hymn may be sung.*

EUCHARISTIC PRAYER

ACCLAMATIONS
*The 'Holy, holy' and 'Christ has died' should be ones that
everyone can join in the singing. For example, those of the
'Israeli Mass'—Hymns Old & New Enlarged, no. 666.*

LORD'S PRAYER
The Spirit of Jesus is poured into our hearts
and helps us to pray together:
Our Father...
*The rest of the Communion rite follows as usual, up to the
fraction. Instead of breaking the bread silently during the
'lamb of God', the celebrant holds up the host clearly, and
says as he breaks it:*
Bread broken,
bread shared
makes us one,
makes us one in Christ.

INVITATION TO COMMUNION
This is Jesus who gives us his Spirit.
Happy are those who are called to his supper.
All: Lord I am not worthy...

During communion, a suitable song may be sung, for example,
♪   *'I am the bread of life'*
Folk Hymnal Volume 2, no. 57;
Hymns Old & New, no. 114;
Hymns Old & New Enlarged, no. 225.
We have received Jesus, we are grateful.
We are grateful too for everyone here
for we give to each other,
we receive from each other.
Let's sing our thanks to God.
A suitable song should be sung, for example,
♪   *'Song of thanksgiving'*
from 'Winter's coming home' (Weston Priory).

PRAYER OF THANKSGIVING
From the rite of confirmation.

CONCLUDING RITES

*The bishop might like to address a few words to the newly
confirmed, their parents, teachers and catechists.*

SOLEMN BLESSING
From the rite of confirmation.

RECESSIONAL
A suitable song may be sung, for example,
♪   *'Walk in the light'*
Songs of the Spirit, no. 15;
Hymns Old & New, no. 273;
Hymns Old & New Enlarged, no. 546.

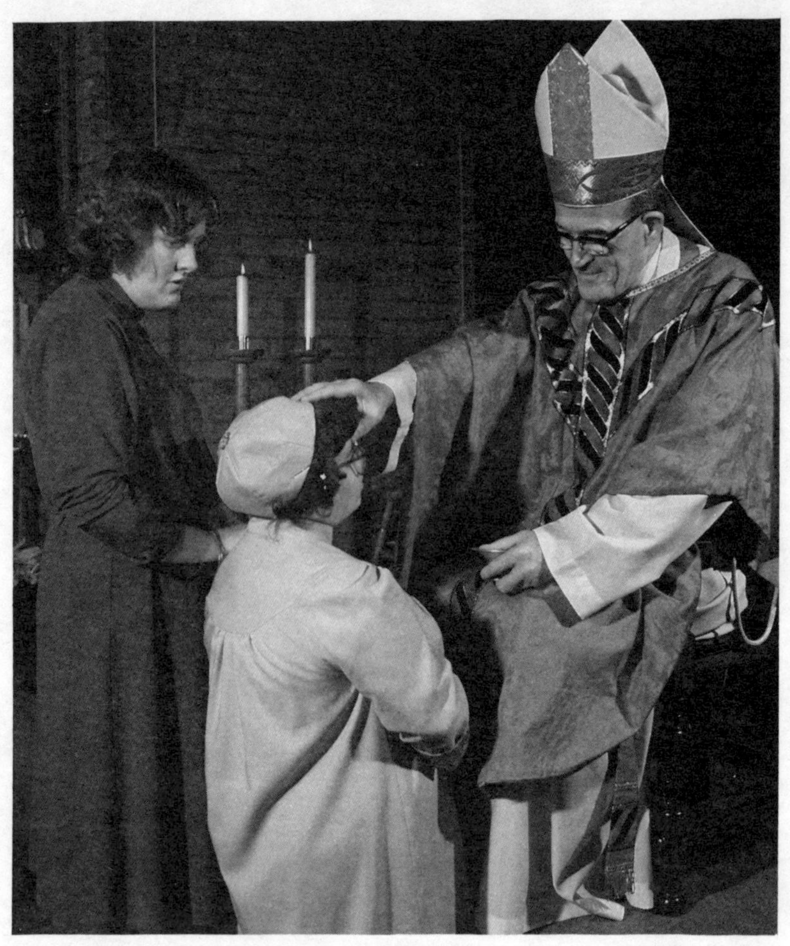

Called to belong.

Part III

FILLED WITH THE SPIRIT

This part is concerned with the practical development of the implications of being confirmed. The effectiveness of such long-term development will depend on the initiative and ingenuity of the group in discovering ways of allowing the confirmed person to exercise a ministry within the local community.

There are many ministries open to the handicapped person: the ministry of welcome; of companionship; of altar serving; of joy; of announcing the Good News.

Through his confirmation the handicapped person has been anointed to continue Christ's work, especially in telling others about God, and in bringing them to God. Only two sessions are offered here, by way of samples.

Session 28   Telling others about God
Session 29   Helping others

TELLING OTHERS ABOUT GOD

AIM
To help the confirmed person become aware that he has been anointed, like Jesus, to tell people about God.

HUMAN EXPERIENCE
   The confirmation ceremony.

SPIRITUAL DIMENSION

   PREPARATION
      For this session you will need:
      —the Book of God's Word;
      —a candle;
      —fresh flowers;
      —appropriate music.
      You will also need photographs or slides of the
      confirmation ceremony.

   RECALL AND DEEPEN THE HUMAN EXPERIENCE
      Through the slides/photographs go over the
      confirmation Mass with the group.
      Recall the significant moments with reference
      to each individual person.
      Help the mentally handicapped person to express
      how they feel.

   CHURCH DIMENSION
      When Bishop… confirmed you, John,
      he made the Sign of the Cross on your forehead
      with holy oil,
      with the oil of Chrism.
      Bishop… made the Sign of the Cross on your
      forehead, Mary.
      Bishop… anointed you with Chrism, Susan.
        Address each one in a similar way.
        Pause.

At our confirmation we were anointed
to show that we say 'Yes' to God.
Being confirmed means
that we want to continue to say 'Yes' to God.
John, you were confirmed.
You want to continue to say 'Yes' to God.
Mary, you were confirmed.
You want to say 'Yes' to God.
  Mention each person—catechist and handicapped.
When we are confirmed
God gives us a special job to do.
God gives Mary a special job to do.
Mary, God wants you to tell everybody about him.
John, God wants you to tell everybody about him.
  Mention each person in the group in a similar way.
  Pause.
God anointed Jesus with the Holy Spirit
and gave him a special job to do.

PROCLAIM THE GOOD NEWS
  Go slowly and deliberately towards the Book
  of God's Word.
  Pick it up with reverence and say:
In the Holy Book we read:
  'The Spirit of the Lord has been given to me
  for he has anointed me.
  He has sent me
  to bring the good news to the poor,
  to proclaim freedom to captives.
  And to the blind new sight,
  to set the downtrodden free,
  to proclaim the Lord's year of favour.'

Luke 4:18-19
& Isaiah 61:1-2

THE MESSAGE
  Go to each person, call them by name and say:
John, Jesus says to you today:
  'Go, tell everyone the Good News.'

RESPONDING TO THE MESSAGE
♪　*'God's Spirit is in my heart.'*
Folk Hymnal Volume 1, no. 57;
Hymns Old & New, no. 89;
Hymns Old & New Enlarged, no. 183.

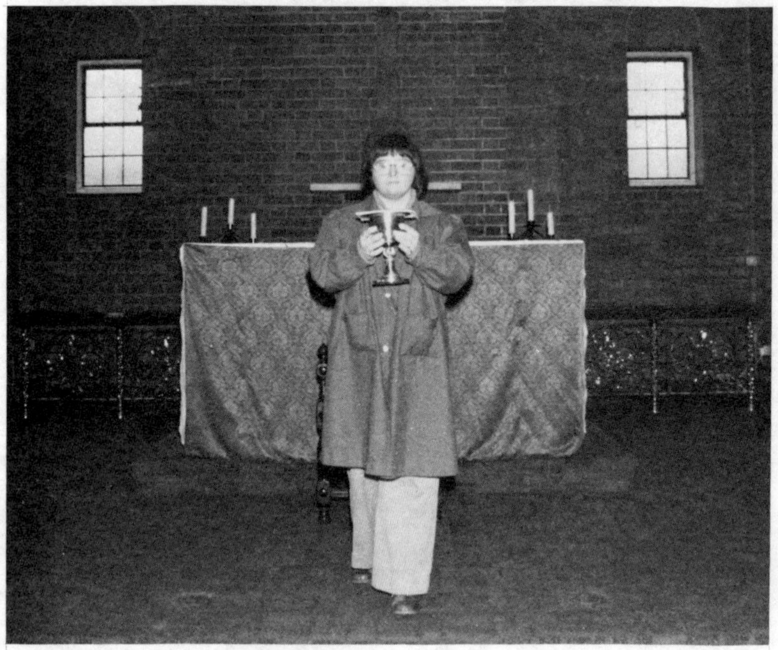

Preparing the chalice for Mass.

Part III Session 29
HELPING OTHERS

AIM

To help the faith community know more deeply that Jesus gives us his Holy Spirit, the gift of His Father's love, so that we can help others.

HUMAN EXPERIENCE

*The involvement of handicapped people in the local
community and their opportunities for carrying out
a specific ministry.*

SPIRITUAL DIMENSION

PREPARATION

*For this session you will need:
—the Book of God's Word;
—a candle;
—fresh flowers.
You will also need something concrete that will evoke
the ministries the handicapped people exercise:
—for example, objects used in their ministry;
—for example, photographs of members of your
    group exercising their ministry.*

RECALL THE HUMAN EXPERIENCE

When I went to Mass on Sunday
I was so pleased to see John
welcoming people at the door with...
Name the appropriate person.
It's good to be welcomed.
It good to have someone to smile at you
as you arrive for Mass.
Mary, did you see John?
Ask each person.
John, looked happy.
You are happy, John, to welcome people to church.
John is helping people to feel welcome.
John is serving all of us in this parish.
John is serving God's people.
Pause.
Look, I have a photograph of Joan.
Look, can you see what she is doing?
Yes, she is cleaning the chalice.
Joan and her friend Susan asked Father...
if they could look after this very special chalice.

I noticed how shiny it was on Sunday.
When the priest held up the chalice
did you notice how beautiful it was, Tom?
> *Ask each person in the group to comment
> if possible.*
Joan is helping all of us.
Joan is serving our parish.
> *Use the different tasks to help them see how they
> help others, how they can share in the church or in
> the local parish.*

DEEPEN THE HUMAN EXPERIENCE

We are happy to help one another.
John is happy to help Mary.
Mary is happy to help Joan.
> *Mention each person.*
We are happy to be able to serve others.
It is good to serve one another.
We feel good.
We feel joined together.
We feel united.

CHURCH DIMENSION

Here around the Book of God's Word we are united.
Here together we are one.
Here we can think about how we serve one another.
in our parish, in our church.
John said 'Yes' to serving others
by welcoming them on Sundays,
Joan said 'Yes' to serving others
by cleaning the chalice we need for Mass.
> *Mention each person in a similar way.*
We all responded to an invitation to serve.
We depend on one another.
Through our serving we are joined together.
We are one.
Our spirits are united.
We are happy to serve, to carry out our ministry.

Here together we listen to one another.
John listens to the rest of us.
Joan listens to the rest of us.
   Address each one.
Together we listen to God's Word.
   Pick up the Book of God's Word reverently and say:
We read from the Book of God's Word.
Jesus speaks to us in the Book of God's Word.
We listen.
Jesus is with us.
The Spirit of Jesus is with us.

PROCLAIM THE GOOD NEWS
In the Holy Book Jesus says:
   'Holy Father keep those you have given me
   true to your name
   so that they may be one like us.
   As you sent me into the world,
   I have sent them into the world.
                                    John 17:11 & 18

THE MESSAGE
   Go to each person, call them by name and say:
John, Jesus says to you today:
   'Go, in my name.
   Serve others.'
   Finally, address the group as a whole:
Jesus says to all of us today:
   'Go in my name.
   Serve others.'

RESPONDING TO THE MESSAGE
   Sing together
   ♪   *'Colours of day'*
Folk Hymnal Volume 2, no. 1;
Hymns Old & New, no. 42;
Hymns Old & New Enlarged, no. 87.

Appendix I

MUSICAL RESOURCES

TITLE	BOOK/LP/CASSETTE	ARTIST/COMPOSER	PUBLISHER/DISTRIBUTOR
Folk Hymnal, Volumes 1-4	Book & Cassette	Various	Kevin Mayhew Ltd
Songs of the Spirit	Book & Cassette	Various	Kevin Mayhew Ltd
More Songs of the Spirit	Book & Cassette	Various	Kevin Mayhew Ltd
Hymns Old & New (333 songs)	Book	Various	Kevin Mayhew Ltd
Hymns Old & New Enlarged (671 songs)	Book	Various	Kevin Mayhew Ltd
I will be with you	LP & Cassette	LaSallian Resource	Kevin Mayhew Ltd
Loving you gently	LP & Cassette	Flame	Kevin Mayhew Ltd
Good morning, Jesus	Book, LP & Cassette	Estelle White	Kevin Mayhew Ltd
Hi God! 1 & 2	Book, LP & Cassette	Carey Landry	NALR (USA) Kevin Mayhew Ltd (UK)
Bloom where you're planted	Book, LP & Cassette	Carey Landry	NALR (USA) Kevin Mayhew Ltd (UK)
I will not forget you	Book, LP & Cassette	Carey Landry	NALR (USA) Kevin Mayhew Ltd (UK)
Abba, Father	Book, LP & Cassette	Carey Landry	NALR (USA) Kevin Mayhew Ltd (UK)
Colour the world with song	Book, LP & Cassette	Carey Landry	NALR (USA) Kevin Mayhew Ltd (UK)

Locusts and wild honey	Book, LP & Cassette	Weston Priory	Weston Priory
Wherever you go	Book, LP & Cassette	Weston Priory	Weston Priory
Listen	Book, LP & Cassette	Weston Priory	Weston Priory
Calm is the night	LP & Cassette	Weston Priory	Weston Priory
Winter's coming home	LP & Cassette	Weston Priory	Weston Priory
	(Book of both of above)		
Spirit alive	Book, LP & Cassette	Weston Priory	Weston Priory
Go up to the mountain	Book, LP & Cassette	Weston Priory	Weston Priory
That there may be bread	Book, LP & Cassette	Weston Priory	Weston Priory
So full of deep joy	Book, LP & Cassette	Weston Priory	Weston Priory
Rise up	Book, LP & Cassette	Weston Priory	Weston Priory
We celebrate reconciliation	LP & Cassette		Silver Burdett (USA) T Shand/Alba Publications (UK)
We celebrate the eucharist	LP & Cassette		Silver Burdett (USA) T Shand/Alba Publications (UK)

Publishers'/Distributors' Addresses:

KEVIN MAYHEW LTD,
55 Leigh Road, Leigh-on-Sea, Essex SS9 1JP. Telephone 0702-76425.

WESTON PRIORY PRODUCTIONS, Weston, Vermont 05161, USA.

T SHAND/ALBA PUBLICATIONS, The Annexe, St Mary's, The Ridgeway, Mill Hill, London NW7.

Appendix II

SPIRITUAL FORMATION BOOKLIST

Useful books for those concerned with the spiritual formation of mentally handicapped people.

I am with you.
Edited by David Wilson, St Paul's Publications (1978).
An introduction into the catechesis of mentally handicapped people.

Life to the full.
Sister Stephanie Clifford, St Joseph's Centre (1980).
An introduction to education in the faith for mentally handicapped children.

Invitation to Communion.
Sister Stephanie Clifford, Kevin Mayhew Ltd (1980).
A First Holy Communion programme for mentally handicapped children.

I meet Jesus.
Jean Vanier, Ann Sigier Publications (1981).

Learning to pray with mentally handicapped.
Sister Jean of the La Retraite Sisters, Kevin Mayhew Ltd (1981).
One of the Getting in touch with God series of booklets.

Belonging.
Sister Stephanie Clifford, St Joseph's Centre (1983).
A programme of catechetical sessions with mentally handicapped people, adaptable to all age groups.

Preparing the Mentally Handicapped for Confirmation.
Rev John Bradford, Church of England Children's Society.
A pamphlet with some valuable insights.